Reminiscences Of Prior Park

James Shepherd

REMINISCENCES

OF

PRIOR PARK.

BY

THE VERY REV.

MONSIGNOR SHEPHERD.

LONDON:
ISAAC PITMAN & SONS, 1 AMEN CORNER, E.C.

1894.

PREFACE.

THE little volume of "Reminiscences," which I published in 1886, is now out of print. A new edition has been called for, and I venture to hope that it will not be less acceptable than its predecessor.

The time which has elapsed since the publication of the first edition, and the information which has been furnished to me by several of those into whose hands it came, has enabled me to correct some inaccuracies, and to fill in many gaps in my narrative. The whole has been carefully re-written.

There are now living only two Ecclesiastics who took part in the foundation of Prior Park College, the Rev. Thomas Albot, of Monmouth, and myself. In a few years there will be no one "left to tell the tale" in its entirety; and therefore, although I am conscious that there may still be some inaccuracies in this book, I have determined to lose no further time in giving to the public a simple and unpretentious record of what I heard and saw of a great Catholic Movement.

It would be idle to affect ignorance that the foundation of Prior Park and the conduct of its Founder have been subjected to severe scrutiny and criticism. It would be vain to deny that the ill-feeling which attended Dr. Baines' action, and the dissension which arose between good and worthy men, have only just sunk into a charitable oblivion.

I am going to say no word to revive the old contention; far rather would I mutilate the tale I have to tell than print a line or a sentence which would give pain to any person or body of persons. When there is strong feeling on either side, it is often difficult for the most conscientious and kindly men to keep their words and actions within due limits; but when acrimony has passed away, things are viewed and discussed in a more favourable light.

Much of what has been said, many things which have been done, have been shown by the test of time to have been well said and well done, which at the time excited eager controversy.

Let me, as a humble follower of that great Prelate, Dr. Baines, testify only that I conscientiously believe that, in all the turmoil of excited controversy and active life, he never took any line without a sincere conviction that it was for the glory of God, and the good of His Church.

To say that he might sometimes have been mistaken, is but to admit that he was human; but many of his views which were at the time most controverted have now been generally adopted.

Corrigenda et Addenda.

Mr. R. E. M. Peach, the author of "Street Lore of Bath," and other works of antiquarian research connected with the city, has given this work a reading during its passage through the press, and kindly furnishes the following notes to the first chapter of Part II.:—

Page 63.—Bishop Warburton occasionally resided at Prior Park. It is said, but the assertion is not supported by evidence, that he remonstrated with Pope for applying the epithet "low-born" to Allen, and that the poet then employed the more gracious term "humble." I believe the change to have been spontaneous on the part of the poet.

Page 64.—The reported discovery by Allen of a suspicious Jacobite correspondence is open to much doubt. There is no allusion to such an event in the annals of the General Post Office.

Page 65.—The Avon was rendered navigable to Bristol through the enterprise of Allen himself, in conjunction with the Duke of Chandos and others.

Page 66.—Wood called the Priory lands which Allen purchased Camulodunum, with a strange misconception of historical facts.

Page 68.—Bishop Warburton died in 1782, and Prior Park then became the residence of the first Viscount Hawarden, who in 1766 married Mary, daughter of Philip Allen and niece of Ralph Allen. His lordship died in 1803, and was succeeded by his son Thomas Ralph, who died in 1807, and all direct connection of Prior Park with the Allen family then came to an end. The property came into the hands of Mr. Thomas, a Bristol merchant and member of the Society of Friends, from whom Dr. Baines purchased the estate.

CONTENTS.

PART I.

PART II.

REMINISCENCES OF PRIOR PARK.

PART I.

CHAPTER I.

PRIOR PARK owes its commencement as a College to the English Benedictine Fathers of Ampleforth, near York. The Right Rev. Peter Baines, Bishop of Siga and Vicar Apostolic of the Western District in England, was himself an English Benedictine monk. He was born at Kirkby, a small village not far from Liverpool, in the spring of 1786. When he was about eleven years of age, he was sent to the English Benedictine Abbey of Lammspring, in Hanover, to pursue his studies for the Church. He remained in this monastery upwards of four years; but on the 6th of April, 1803, the Abbey with its territory (some twenty-six miles in circumference) was seized and formally occupied by the Prussian Government. Monks and students were obliged to return, as best they could, to England. After a few months spent with his parents, he repaired to Ampleforth, where a monastery and college had just been started by the Benedictine Fathers from Lammspring. At the age of twenty-four, Peter Augustine Baines was ordained priest—Augustine being his name in religion. Not long after his ordination he was appointed to the Benedictine Mission at Bath. In 1823, Father Baines was named Co-adjutor to Bishop Collingridge, and was consecrated in Dublin, on the 1st of May, in the same year. During the next three years Dr. Baines was so zealous in the government of the Western District, that at last his health broke down, and he was obliged to leave his duties in England and travel on the Continent.

In his "Recollections of the Last Four Popes," Cardinal Wiseman says :—

"In the winter of 1826, there arrived in Rome, the Right Rev. Dr. Baines, Bishop of Siga and Co-adjutor of the English Western District. He came in a state of almost hopeless illness, with an interior abscess working on an enfeebled frame and constitution, apparently unable to expel it from the system. He came merely as a visitor, with some private friends, who had kindly accompanied him, in hopes that change of climate might do more than medicines, or their administrators. They were not deceived. The mild climate, the interesting recreation, and perhaps more still, the rest from the labour and excitement, in which he had lived, did their duty; at some due period, the interior enemy capitulated in that Englishman's stronghold of misery and pain—the liver; and a visible change for the better was observable by spring. A delightful summer, spent between Assisi and Porto di Fermo, completed the task of recovery."

He had then every opportunity, not only of reestablishing his health, but of improving his natural taste for the good, the beautiful, and the sublime in religion and the fine arts. How much he developed the elegant taste, with which he was gifted, is, to a certain extent, apparent to this day in the arrangement and disposal of the college and grounds of Prior Park.

In the summer of 1828, Dr. Baines stayed for some time at the Benedictine Monastery of Subiaco; and shortly before the death of Leo XII. in the February of 1829, the learned and courtly English Bishop was appointed by the Pope, a domestic chaplain at the Vatican. Two months later, on March 3rd, Bishop Collingridge died, and Dr. Baines had to hasten back to England to take up the reins of government in the Western District.

England has now, thank God, a complete Hierarchy: Bishops and Heads of Religious Houses, Secular and Regular Parish Priests, labour in the vineyard, each with well-defined and understood duties and prerogatives. They are agreed, not only in the end to be attained, but as to the means to be employed to reach it.

In the year 1829, things were very different. Catholic Emancipation had only just been wrung from an unwilling Minister and a reluctant Monarch. The Members of Religious Orders could not follow their different rules with any approach to exactitude. They had but just emerged from a state of active persecution, and were glad in being allowed to follow their sacred ministry unmolested. Few Missions had resident Priests.

All honour to the noble band of Secular and Regular Missionaries who had tended the lamp of faith during the terrible half-century which preceded the establishment of the Hierarchy! But it was a natural consequence of the mode in which Ecclesiastical affairs had, perforce of circumstances, to be administered, that considerable disorder and confusion prevailed. Rights and interests overlapped; difficulties of all sorts arose, such as are now impossible. It was on all hands admitted that great changes must be introduced; and in the absence of any regular Canonical system, what wonder that good men, and wise men, differed as to what those changes ought to be.

Dr. Baines was a man of large mind and great breadth of view. He knew how things were in England—he knew the then status and organisation of the English Benedictine congregation—and he had had the great advantage of a lengthened sojourn in Rome, and of free communication and interchange of views with the greatest Prelates of the day.

His grand idea was the foundation of a great Ecclesiastical Seminary for Priests in the South-Western District, under the immediate supervision of the Bishop; and of a College for Catholic youths of the upper classes, such as might raise the whole tone of Catholicity. He felt that Catholics had been so long oppressed that they had become depressed, and that it was necessary to show the nation that they lacked neither the capacity nor the spirit to take their proper share of public life.

Such a plan required for its execution a fine building and a capable staff.

As regarded the building, circumstances were

propitious. The Mansion at Prior Park had been built by the celebrated architect Wood for Ralph Allen, just at the period of the Renaissance of the City of Bath. Magnificent in design, noble in structure, almost unique in its advantages of situation, it appeared such a building as was manifestly required. There was also a prestige about the place, which fitted it for Dr. Baines' purpose almost as much as did its more material advantages. It was pre-eminently the Mansion House of Bath. It had been the residence of Allen when he was, in a far truer sense than that attributed to Beau Nash, "the King of Bath." He had held his court there—Bishop Warburton, the poet Pope, the novelist Fielding, were but *three* of the literary men who adorned it.

Any Institution claiming its home in Prior Park might be liked or disliked; it could not be ignored.

The Estate was a considerable one (186a. 2r. 37p.) and was purchased for £22,000. This was in December, 1829. It was natural for Dr. Baines, in considering the personnel of a teaching staff, to look to the College of Ampleforth—to the men whom he knew and trusted, and over whom he had presided.

The exact circumstances—the steps in the general line of Dr. Baines' conduct—which led to an exodus from Ampleforth to Prior Park have been much canvassed; and for the reasons given in the preface I do not propose to lift the veil which partly shrouds the episode. But this may be said—Ampleforth was then in rather low circumstances—changes in the administration of the

English Benedictine congregation were imminent, and there was grave doubt as to the validity of the vows under which the Religious lived. Bishop Baines visited the College of Ampleforth as soon as he had completed the purchase of Prior Park. He stated his views, and they met with general approbation amongst the Superiors and Religious there. The personal attractions of Bishop Baines were peculiarly great, and this I am convinced was a great factor in the whole arrangement. Indeed, to anyone not taking this into consideration, the story would seem almost incredible.

Cardinal Wiseman, in his "Recollections of the Last Four Popes," says :—"He had a power of fascinating all who approached him ; on every subject he had a command of language, and a clear manner of expressing himself which secured attention and generally won assent. Hence his acquaintances were always willing listeners, and soon became sincere admirers, and then warm partisans."

From my experience, I can testify to the truth of what is here stated about Dr. Baines. His appearance as he entered the Sanctuary at Ampleforth in Cappa Magna, and took his position in his sedilia to preach to us, was very imposing—the more so, perhaps, because we were quite unaccustomed to it. His sermons to this day remain deeply impressed on my mind. What Cardinal Wiseman says of the Bishop's preaching in Rome is exactly what I myself wish to say of his preaching at Ampleforth College :—"The flow of his words was easy and copious, his imagery was often very elegant, and his discourses were replete with thought and solid matter. But his great power was in his delivery—in voice, in tone, in look, in gesture. His whole manner was full of pathos; there was a peculiar tremulousness of voice, which gave his words more than double effect. He was considered, by all that heard him, one of the most eloquent and earnest preachers they had ever listened to." The prestige which he enjoyed before he came amongst us also tended to enhance the awe and respect with which we regarded him; for Pope Leo XII. had taken preliminary steps to making him a Cardinal. Dr. Baines had been desired to remove from his private apartments in the Palazzo Costa, where he had been living with his English friends, to the Benedictine Monastery of San Callisto, and to wear the episcopal habit of his Order.

Bishop Baines was awaiting further directions, when death interfered with the completion of the design by calling Pope Leo. XII. to another world.

A sojourn of three years in Italy and other foreign countries had enabled Dr. Baines thoroughly to master the different systems pursued abroad in the education of ecclesiastical students. He was familiar with the pontifical functions at St. Peter's; he was well versed in the antiquities and architectural beauties of Rome; and his conversations on these subjects were highly entertaining and instructive.

Mr. Frederick Lucas, the Editor of the *Tablet*, on hearing of Bishop Baines' death, amongst other things, said:—"No one could be in Bishop Baines' company for a quarter of an hour without seeing that he was emphatically 'a man;' a man of high heart; robust and masculine understanding; a dignity at once majestic and homely—that is, wholly free from the least shadow of littleness or affectation; full of good sense, directness of purpose, lofty courage, a penetration before which meaner natures quailed, and a cheerful and sportive humour, which often in words seemingly unstudied, half jest and half earnest, sent forth utterances of singular and profound wisdom. His manner, like his mind, was peculiarly artless. In his most careless conversation, as well as in his more studied discourses and in his writings, his words dropped from him sweet as honey and soft as a stream of oil; but nothing that he said or wrote ever smelt of the lamp. He was graceful and beautiful in discourse, because it was his nature to be so, and he could only have become otherwise by affectation and effort; and yet this grace was rendered even more piquant and attractive by a certain genial homeliness, which took from it every appearance of effeminacy; and woe to those who, mistaking the glass-like smoothness of his weapon, presumed to trifle with its edge. It was essentially a manly grace; not an outward trick of manner, but the unstudied effusion of the heart; and accompanied by a certain childlike simplicity and unpretending wisdom that made honest men, even if they were at odds with him, to reverence him and pay him tribute of their unsuspected praise. His disposition was kindness itself: ardent and occasionally hasty, but placable at a word, and without a trace of malice or ill-will. He was prompt, as most of our readers know—and as we know in particular—to administer reproof where it was deserved and needed. But as he gave his advice and admonition with the frankness of one who means well and fears no misconstruction, so he was ready to receive with a like frankness and an unconscious humility all suggestions and advice that seemed to issue from a good, even if an ill-placed, intention. To come back to our old expression, he was essentially 'a man'—well-proportioned, great, active, and born for high achievements. It may seem presumptuous in us to pretend to describe this illustrious person's character, clumsily it may be, and with a vain effort at precision; but with one or two exceptions, in which we have been guided by what we consider sure authority, we have here set down nothing which is not drawn from the image of him impressed by a short and sharp process upon our own minds. There are some persons whom you seem to know more intimately in a quarter of an hour than you do others after years of acquaintance. And so it was with Dr. Baines. Great as he was, an humble visitor seemed to see him and understand him at once, and that, precisely, because he *was* great, simple, and natural. In our humble judgment, too, he well understood the Catholic body, and was admirably fitted to be its leader."

No wonder, then, that the inmates of Ampleforth College, and particularly the young men, were anxious to place themselves under the direction of so experienced a guide, and to avail themselves of the advantageous offers which he made them ; and not only the young and enthusiastic, but even the older inmates of the College were animated by the same spirit—and a species of exodus from Ampleforth to Prior Park was contemplated.

The action taken by the Benedictine Authorities is outside the limits within which I wish to confine myself, viz., the writing my "Reminiscences" of the past in connection, as far as possible, with Prior Park only.

I wish, then, to state that the Prior of Ampleforth, the Sub-Prior, and the Procurator were found willing to co-operate in founding the College of Prior Park. Their names were the Very Rev. Thomas Burgess (afterwards Bishop of Clifton), the Rev. Thomas Rooker, and the Rev. Edward Metcalfe. Three of the Novices volunteered their services, viz., Leonard Calderbank, Moses Furlong, and Peter Hutton. Upwards of twenty students also left Ampleforth at the same time and went to Prior Park. The Ecclesiastical students were James Abraham, Thomas Abbot, Ralph Brindle, James Baines, Jacob Illingworth, James Shepherd (myself), John Bonomi, William Agar, and Luke Metcalfe. Amongst the Lay students were Charles Hugh Clifford, five sons of Sir Edward Mostyn, Bart. (of Falacre Hall), Vincent Gandolfi, Charles Slaughter, and others. That the Superiors of Ampleforth College became the first Superiors of Prior Park, under Bishop Baines, and that the Novices became the first teachers at Prior Park, are facts which I simply wish to record—and without comment. That these Superiors transferred their obedience to Dr. Baines and left the English Benedictine Order is also a fact on which I make no further remark—everything having been done with the sanction of His Holiness Pope Leo XII. That the movement gave rise to much discussion and misunderstanding may be easily imagined ; but seeing that Ampleforth College has flourished notwithstanding the exodus to Prior Park, we may well confine ourselves to admiring the ways of Divine Providence which, without materially injuring one College, has made it the means of establishing another.

Some very curious mis-statements have been current as to some supposed abstraction of property from Ampleforth by those who migrated to Prior Park. These are backed upon a complete misconception of the facts. A commission was nominated to investigate the matter, and Dr. Baines was absolved from all blame.

The documents will be found set out in Appendix No. 1.

To the staff of Professors from Ampleforth were soon added others from Rome. Foremost among these was Dr. Logan, an eminent mathematician and thinker, who, on account of his great learning, was for many years in receipt of £100 per annum from the "Queen's Bounty." Previous to his reception into the Catholic Church, he had been instructed in the faith by Bishop Baines himself. He was ordained priest at Prior Park, and taught mathematics until he went to Oscott, of which he became the President.

In the very early days of Prior Park, the studies were conducted mainly by Dr. Rooker, Dr. Toomey, Dr. Logan, and the Novices from Ampleforth (Fathers Furlong and Hutton). The first Prefect at Prior Park was Father O'Dwyer. But no names are so conspicuous, as Prefects and Presidents of both Colleges, as those of Fathers Furlong and Hutton. They were both disciplinarians, and Father Hutton, as a master, carried to his task a great love of labour, a thorough acquaintance with his duties, and a keen sense of his responsibility.

About this time, Thomas Shattock (whose declining years were spent at St. Mary's, Bath, and who was much respected as a member of the Clifton Chapter) came from St. Acheul, driven back to England by the revolution which deprived Charles X. of his throne. Canon Shattock related to me how, during the revolution, the inmates of St. Acheul were collected together before a statue of Our Blessed Lady, in the grounds of the Seminary, reciting her Litany, when some of the mob mounted the garden wall, with loaded rifles in their hands ; but instead of making glorious martyrs of the priests and students, as they anticipated, the rabble went quietly away, leaving them under the protection of Her whose aid they were invoking. The staff of Superiors and Professors was also recruited from the Members of another Religious Order, the Institute of Charity. Bishop Baines, visiting the North of Italy in September, 1834, called upon the Abbate Rosmini, who had gathered around him several pious and learned men, the nucleus of the Institute of Charity, which was afterwards sanctioned at Rome by Pope Gregory XVI., December 20th, 1838. Foremost amongst these holy and learned men were the Rev. Dr. Gentili, John Baptist Pagani, Antonio Rey, Emile Belisy, Rinolfi, and Signini. His Lordship petitioned the Abbate Rosmini to send these distinguished Ecclesiastics, with three Lay brothers, to assist him in carrying on his work in England. To this the Abbate Rosmini consented; and three of the above-mentioned Members of the Institute of Charity reached England on June 15th, 1835. These were the Rev. Dr. Gentili, Don Antonio Rey, and Emile Belisy, the two latter being Frenchmen. The others followed two years later, in 1837, viz., the Rev. John Baptist Pagani, Rinolfi, and Fortunatus Signini, and three Lay brothers (all Italians). Dr. Gentili was ubiquitous. He was the President of St. Paul's, taught philosophy, gave lectures in St. Peter's, got up Italian plays and concerts, preached continually, and was the Spiritual Director of the whole house. Father Pagani was an eminent theologian and ascetic, and had taught large classes in Italy. The Rev. Antonio Rey was "a walking library of theology," and the Rev. Belisy, Rinolfi, and Signini were employed in teaching the modern languages—French, Italian, and German.

Such an accession of teaching power soon produced very salutary effects. But more striking, perhaps, were the changes of life, for the better, which were brought about in the College, by the exhortations and good example of these holy and learned Religious. These changes were mainly consequent upon a course of spiritual exercises, preached during Passion Week in the year 1836 by Dr. Gentili. During the Retreat, which was attended by the whole College—Professors and students—the spiritual exercises of St. Ignatius were followed, the horarium was drawn up, and strict silence was enjoined. With a crucifix on his breast, Dr. Gentili preached several times a day from a platform raised in the Chapel. In those days, Retreats of this kind were a novelty; and the rigid discipline enforced, gave rise at first to some criticism and murmuring; but soon the energy and effect, with which the preacher announced the awful truths of eternity, aided by Divine grace, operated upon the hearts of his hearers, producing great recollection and compunction of spirit. The good results of the Retreat were of a lasting nature.

One of Dr. Gentili's converts was Mr. Henry Field, a distinguished musician and eminent pianist. The good Doctor commenced this work of conversion by entering into friendly conversation with Mr. Field on the musical compositions of the celebrated Rossini; and they spoke particularly of the air in the opera of the "Barbiere di Seviglia" commencing with the words, "Largo al Factotum della citta." This was the air which Gentili used to sing (as he said in a letter describing the event) "when he was a fool in the midst of the world." By degrees he led the musician from profane to sacred music, and thence to the subject of religion. This he did so effectually that Mr. Field finished by resolving to make his general confession on Our Blessed Lady's festival, the Presentation A.D. 1835. After having been duly prepared, Bishop Baines received him as a Member of the Catholic Church on the feast of St. Cecilia, the patroness of music and song. Mr. Henry Field's conversion was thorough. He left his residence in Bath, and occupied a white-washed room, without a fireplace, at the end of the top gallery in St. Paul's—the last room on the right-hand side. Like a Religious, he seemed to delight in his cell, and was a devout frequenter of the Holy Sacrament. The gallery was filled with secular students, Father William Eyre, S.J., for many years Rector of Stonyhurst, being one of them. Mr. Field's presence amongst them was useful in imparting a gentlemanly tone of thought and action, whilst his splendid performances on the piano were an endless source of refined amusement.

All things were proceeding harmoniously and prosperously between the Bishop and the Members of the Institute of Charity at Prior Park, when there arose a subject of disagreement. It was evident that the arrangement by which the Members of a religious Institute were to take an active part in the teaching work of a College, governed by secular Superiors, could not be of a permanent character. The secular Professors who were working under Dr. Baines, and who looked in all things solely to his authority and counsel, formed a distinct body by themselves. To introduce into the working of the establishment a number of foreign Professors, whose obedience was claimed chiefly and primarily by an outside Ecclesiastic, however eminent he might be, was bringing in an altogether heterogeneous element. It is true that the Members of the Society were expressly and frequently commanded by the Superior General to yield on all occasions a most loyal and willing obedience in matters regarding the collegiate work of the establishment. Of these lessons and admonitions, the following extract will suffice as an illustration. It is taken from a letter written by Rosmini to Dr. Gentili, and runs as follows :—"Do everything in your power to comply with the Bishop's desires, preferring them to charitable works of supererogation. Charge yourselves, therefore, with nothing that can interfere with your engagements to His Lordship, or that is likely to give him umbrage." Nor were these injunctions from Rosmini ill attended to, as is evinced by the commendatory letter which Dr. Baines sent to the Abbate, and in which he expresses his high admiration of the Fathers of Charity.

The circumstances which led to the final separation were such as were quite beyond the control of either party. At the same time the Fathers of Charity were obedient and submissive to Dr. Baines, they could not, and what is more, they ought not to have forgotten that they were the members of a religious Order. The obligations which they were called upon to fulfil appertained to their position, not only as masters in a collegiate staff, but also as members of a religious body, with duties and requirements distinctly its own. In a letter from the Abbate Rosmini to his subjects at Prior Park, we read that they must not, to please Dr. Baines, do anything contrary to the spirit or essential rules of the Institute, maintaining that independence necessary for its very existence, and the good it proposes to effect. The very spirit which animated them, the external functions which, by their rule, they had to perform day after day, all combined to set them apart as a body of men who, whatever might be their good intentions, led to a distinct, and to a certain extent isolated, existence in the College itself. The consequences are easily foreseen. There soon began to exist between the Bishop and the Members of the Institute a state of feeling which, compatible with genuine friendship and mutual esteem and affection, yet at the same time was so delicate, that but little was wanted to change this feeling into one of positive divergence and separation. There are two things which more particularly brought about this result. The first is that some of the most conspicuous and able members of Dr. Baines' staff manifested a desire to join the Institute of Charity. With this view, they expressly asked the Bishop to allow them to transfer their allegiance, from him to the Abbate Rosmini. Their request was complied with. But the Bishop began to fear that others also, perhaps even the greater part of his subjects, might express a similar wish, and that, thus, he would be left dependent for the prosperity of the College and district committed to his care upon the good-will of the Superiors of the Society of Charity.

The first symptom of an altered state of mind on his part, was the removal of Dr. Gentili from the College, to another part of the Diocese. As Dr. Gentili was the Superior of the Members at the College, this occasioned no small amount of embarrassment, both to the Fathers at the College and the Abbate Rosmini. The separation was of such long duration that the latter was obliged to appoint a new Superior. He accordingly notified the same to Dr. Gentili, who was requested to give, in person, a letter containing the instructions he deemed opportune in this altered state of things. He returned to Prior Park for this purpose, and having assembled his brethren, with a countenance expressive of interior joy at being relieved from so great a responsibility, he himself read the decree of his own deposition and the election of a new Superior. After giving them a brief and edifying discourse, he knelt down, and asking pardon of God and his brethren for the defects committed during the government of the College, he requested the new Superior to impose a penance upon him, and before rising, kissed the feet of all the brethren.

The appointment of a new Superior, however, did not improve matters; and the position of the Fathers in the College was becoming daily more untenable. Their Meditations and frequent religious exercises were as so many acts of an influential body of men, calculated in themselves to win others over to their ranks, and hence, evidently, prejudicial to the welfare of the College itself. The support and patronage which Lady Arundell gave to the Fathers, increasing, as it did, this unwelcome influence, rendered things still more critical. We must, however, carefully refrain from attributing this apparent distrust on the part of the Bishop to any personal motives. His conversations with Father E. Belisy, published in the "Lady Arundell Memoirs," contained in the Ratclifton, show that the mind of Dr. Baines oscillated between two opposite and conflicting opinions. One day he is represented as expressing a wish that the Fathers of Charity were removed altogether from the teaching staff of the College, and on the next entirely disclaiming any such wish. The truth is that while his esteem and affection for the Fathers of Charity naturally led him to make a continued use of their services, he was at the same time actuated by the fear of being rendered completely dependent upon them. At length, the crisis came, and one by one the Fathers were removed from this first field of their labours in England.

CHAPTER II.

History of the College to the Departure of the Fathers of Charity.

THE staff of Religious Professors under Father Pagani's direction, with the accession of the English members, was very considerable. These resided at St. Paul's College, of which Canon Shattock was the President, in the place of Dr. Gentili. Father Furlong was the Vice-President of St. Paul's, whilst Father Hutton took the lead at St. Peter's. All things seemed to prosper, and the studies in both colleges were in a flourishing condition. I have now before me a printed prospectus of the examination of the students and distribution of prizes, A.D. 1842. The heading of the prospectus is as follows:—

"PRIOR PARK, BATH.

"Quod bonum faustum felixque sit, rei litterariae benevertat, publicantur nomina adolescentium qui in Collegiis Principum Apostolorum Petri et Pauli, facto disciplinarum ac litterarum experimento, suffragiis Censorum, et Reverendissimi Episcopi Sigensis decreto, proemia et laudes publice consecuti sunt, IV. Idus Juli, Anno MDCCCXLII."

Examinations were held in the following subjects:—Theology, Scripture, Philosophy, Rhetoric, Natural Philosophy, Chemistry, Geometry, Algebra, Trigonometry, Music, Drawing, Elocution, Greek, Latin, French, German, and Italian. The name most conspicuous is that of Louis English, afterwards Rector of the English College at Rome, and to whom the "Collegio Pio" was mainly indebted for its existence. On this occasion, he took almost all the first prizes. Many other names are honourably mentioned of boys whom I remember with affectionate regard :—Hercy, Bateman, Chichester, Guibara, O'Connor, Coxon, etc. Whilst mentioning names, a word may be said of students of anterior date whose names reflect the highest credit on the College. Foremost among them is Ferdinand English, eventually Archbishop of Trinidad. Bishop Baines, writing to Mrs. English, said, "Your son Ferdinand is in many respects decidedly the first student in the English College, and, if he goes on as he has begun, will do great credit to his friends." That he did go on as he began we learn from a paragraph in the *Tablet* :—"On Monday, Sept. 4th, the annual distribution of prizes took place in the hall of the Roman Seminary. The students of the English College kept up their reputation. Mr. Ferdinand English (Western District) was created Doctor in Theology, with universal applause, having passed his examination with that high success which was expected from his talents and application. He also carried away the gold medal of pre-eminence amongst those who were created Doctors in Theology." Of Louis English, Cardinal Manning, writing a letter of condolence to the Countess English, who was his sister, on the occasion of his death, said, "I feel that I have lost a dear and valued friend; and the Church has lost a man who promised more than any man of his age I know amongst us." He died at the age of 37, A.D. 1863. Bishop Ullathorne, writing on the same melancholy occasion and to the same person, said:—"As having known much of your departed brother, because I was his Bishop when he was a student in Rome, I have some little right to speak of him. He was a truly interior man—a man of self-denial and prayer. His principles were of that high character which always win intuition into the sound side of great questions. He was entirely unselfish. He was greatly respected and looked up to by those who had been his pupils. He was prudent and peaceful. He looked to the cultivation of the soul before that of the intellect, and cultivated the intellect upon the highest and most loyal principles. The Pope appreciated him, and it was the personal wish of His Holiness to place him in the position which he held as the head of the English College in Rome." It was Dr. Louis English who, when walking with his sister, the Countess English, saw two young men coming down Park Street, Bristol, and turning to her said, "I wish to introduce these two young men to you; they will do good in the Church." The two young men were Messrs. Edward and James Williams. With these two names I would couple the name of William Clifford, the beloved and learned Bishop of the Diocese of Clifton; and I do so because by their united efforts they performed the memorable feat of raising and floating a stranded vessel—none other than the magnificent twin ship of SS. Peter and Paul at Prior Park. His Lordship had been both student and prefect in the College. I would also mention the name of another of the former students, Henry Clifford, who served his country so well, earning for himself the rank and title of General in the British Army, and gaining the rare distinction of the Victoria Cross. Finally, not to be tedious, let me mention the name of Arthur Herbert, now General Herbert. He was the companion in arms of his fellow-collegian General Sir Henry Clifford during the Crimean War. He once related to me how he had prepared himself for death by receiving Holy Communion previous to leading a storming party against Sebastopol; and yet his companions and friends will be glad to learn that the hero of many fights has never been so much as even slightly wounded. Other notable students might be introduced.

But I am wandering from my subject. I was speaking of the examination and the distribution of prizes in the summer of 1842. The number of students brought forward for that public exhibition, and whose names are printed in the prospectus, is seventy. How many smaller boys there were I do not know; but it is more than probable that there were many boys at the College at the time whose names do not appear, particularly as the numbers at one time reached more than one hundred. Numbers have much to do with the prosperity of a College, and all things considered, these may be deemed to have been the palmy days of Prior Park.

If, however, at this period Prior Park was at its zenith, it was also the period at which it began to decline. Its excellent Professors were disappearing from the scene as in a dissolving view—not all at once, but still completely. The Rev. Don Antonio Rey went to teach theology in America, and the Rev. Father Pagani went to Ratcliffe College. The Rev. Fathers Belisy, Rinolfi, and Signini were invited by Bishop Walsh, of Birmingham, to take possession of "Old Oscott" and to teach in the new College, which had been recently erected. Fathers Furlong and Hutton went to Italy. There was another source of dissatisfaction also, arising from the fact that the Fathers of the Institute of Charity had alienated from Dr. Baines and Prior Park the good wishes and interest of Lady Mary Arundell of Wardour and daughter of the Duke of Buckingham. After the restoration of the Mansion, which had been destroyed by fire on May 31st, 1836, this good Lady took up her abode in the best rooms of the Mansion, and was instrumental in furnishing very suitably the same apartments that I now occupy. This was between the years 1839 and 1842. Owing to an arrangement made to the effect that the furniture should, under any circumstances, belong to the College, it came to pass that it was all sold, with the rest of the property, in liquidation of the College liabilities, the execution coming off, as will be hereafter mentioned, January 1st, 1856. The rooms are, however, once more handsomely furnished.

The Hon. Miss Crewe was residing at the

Priory, and the two ladies were bosom friends and constant companions. Miss Crewe was a devoted friend of Prior Park, and the Bishop fully expected that Lady Arundell would be the same. But the influence of the Members of the Institute over Her Ladyship proved too strong for the Bishop. She allowed herself to be entirely guided by the Fathers, and hence arose a feeling of jealousy which tended to make the position of the Fathers painful in the College, and Father Pagani was the first to look out for a new home for the Institute of Charity. After some correspondence between the Father General Rosmini and Bishop Walsh, of the Midland District, "Mary Vale" or "Old Oscott" was occupied by the Fathers who had left Prior Park. These same Professors became the Professors at the new Seminary of Oscott. In the meantime, Lady Arundell, who had become one of the "Ascribed Members" of the Institute of Charity, had left Prior Park for Loughborough, where she established the first Convent of the Sisters of Providence in England. Here she died a holy and edifying death A.D. 1845.

At the close of May, Lady Mary was seized with a violent internal inflammation, and suffered most fearfully agonising pains for two days. She was attended night and day by the Sisters, and the Fathers of Charity were in continual attendance, encouraging her to patience, and administering all the consolations of religion. During the whole time, Lady Mary Arundell gave the greatest edification by her humility and patient resignation. She expressed the consolation that she experienced from being thus assisted in her last trying moments by holy Religious. On account of constant sickness, she was unable to receive the holy Viaticum; but, after making her confession, she received the holy Sacrament of Extreme Unction, and calmly breathed her last on the morning of the 2nd of June, 1845.

It was her holy wish to be buried like a poor woman, and that no mark of her high rank should be exhibited in her funeral. This wish was complied with as far as was possible.

The funeral took place on Saturday, June 7, the Feast of St. John Nepomucen, martyr. Though there was a total absence of all worldly pomp, yet it was, probably, the most solemn funeral that has been witnessed in England since the schism of the sixteenth century.

Over the remains of Lady Arundell was placed a thick polished slab of slate, on which, beneath one of Pugin's beautifully floriated crosses in brass, and over a shield emblazoned with her arms, may be read in the Church of Ratcliffe College the following epitaph :—

ORATE PRO ANIMA MARIÆ ANNÆ
GEORGII MARCHIONIS
BUCKINGENSIS FILIÆ, JACOBI
EVERARDI BARONUM
ARUNDELL DE WARDOUR VIDUÆ, QUÆ
RELIGIONE, PIETATE ET PRÆSERTIM
CHARITATE ERGA PAUPERES
CONSPICUA, DIE II. JUNII A.D.
MDCCCXLV., ÆTATIS VERO SUÆ LVIII.,
IN SANCTA PACE QUIEVIT.

But to return. The "end all" centred in Fathers Furlong and Hutton. They had been Dr. Baines' support from the beginning—his Presidents, his Prefects, his Teachers—and to give them up was to surrender his last stronghold. All might depart, but not those old friends. His Lordship heard of their intended departure, and through his nephew, the Rev. James Baines, he sent them a written command to remain at their posts. The practical answer to this peremptory order was that with or without the Bishop's leave they would go—and away they went to Italy. Thus, before the death of Bishop Baines in July, 1843, the Institute of Charity became extinct at Prior Park.

Here again we may pause to consider the wonderful ways of Divine Providence in supplying labourers for the restoration of the faith amongst us. Prior Park received the Members of the Institute of Charity into its bosom, when, with the exception of Father Gentili, none could understand or speak the English language. During their stay at Prior Park, they prepared themselves most efficiently for the great works which they afterwards accomplished, viz., the foundation of a College at Ratcliffe (near Leicester), a Noviciate at Rugby, and flourishing Missions in England and Wales. To some of these Missions are attached Sisters of Providence of the same Order, to teach the schools and assist the poor. Prior Park also furnished a Superior for life to Ratcliffe College in the person of Father Hutton, formerly President of St. Peter's College. Father Hutton was an accomplished Classical and English scholar, a good mathematician, a powerful thinker, a good theologian and preacher. It furnished also a companion to Father Gentili in Father Furlong, who became, with him, an itinerant Catholic Missionary. In imitation of Christ and His Apostles, they were for years employed in travelling from place to place preaching the Word of God, according to the method in use among the popular Missionaries of Italy. The good which these Missionaries did is incalculable, and not wholly unknown to the inhabitants of Bath and Bristol. Father Furlong, from his long experience in the management of boys at Prior Park, became, after Dr. Gentili's death, a very successful founder and manager of a reformatory in Ireland. Nor were the benefits conferred upon Prior Park by the Fathers by any means inconsiderable. They promoted religious devotion among the masters and students, introduced a greater spirit of discipline and subordination, and fostered to a greater extent the study of the ancient and modern languages. Nor was this all. When the good fame of Bishop Baines was impugned at Rome, and complaints had been launched against the Professors of the College, it was Father Gentili who, writing to the Holy Father, laid bare the true facts of the case, and changed the voice of disapprobation into one of praise and commendation. If mutual good services are capable of fostering mutual affection and esteem, surely the perusal of the history of the past should revive similar sentiments, since it was owing to their collateral energy and assistance that Prior Park and the Institute of Charity became, in the earlier part of this century, the great pioneers of Catholic truth in England.

CHAPTER III.

Dr. Baines is Summoned to Rome.

IN the month of May, 1840, Dr. Baines called his Professors together and informed us that he had been suddenly and unexpectedly called to Rome. An official letter from Propaganda gave him to understand that affairs of the highest importance, which were then under consideration at Rome, indispensably required his presence in the capital of the Catholic world.

In obedience to this summons, His Lordship left us on the 19th of May and arrived in Rome on the 9th of June. On the following day, he presented himself to the Prefect of the Propaganda, and to his Secretary, but without receiving the slightest hint as to why he had been sent for; and it was not until the 2nd of July that His Eminence the Cardinal Prefect and Most Reverend Secretary read to him certain charges which had been made against his Lental Pastoral, and which he was called upon to answer.

The Pastoral had been denounced by accusers unknown to Bishop Baines. No Vicar Apostolic had found fault with it; on the contrary, Bishop Briggs especially approved of it. But it had not found favour with a certain class of converts whose mistaken zeal had led them to take upon themselves to reform the Church in exterior matters: for instance, an attempt was being made to change the sacred vestments, liturgy, and ceremonial of Rome, and to introduce others which were supposed to have been used at some former period in England. For this purpose, the chasuble was to be nearly six feet in width, and to hang in ample folds before and behind. The Communion rail was to be omitted in the new Churches, the Tabernacle was to be dispensed with, and the Blessed Sacrament was to be suspended from the ceiling by a chain or cord in a silver dove. On Good Friday, the Consecrated Host was to be inserted in the breast of a full-sized wooden or stone figure of our Saviour in the tomb, and the faithful were to watch before it till Easter Sunday. The Roman Missal was to be set aside and the old English Missal of Salisbury substituted in its place—and so forth. Dr. Baines, having had the advantage of assisting for several years at the throne of the Sovereign Pontiff, could not but appreciate the *Papal* ceremonial, and he was convinced that it was well suited to England, and needed no reform.

He, therefore, undertook to oppose the innovation by the power of his Episcopal authority. This his preference to the Roman ritual it was, together with other points of discipline and doctrine, that brought His Lordship into trouble.

To me who knew Bishop Baines so well, it is impossible to believe that he was disliked by converts *in general.* He was the *one* Bishop, who by his sermons and writings had done the most for religion in England. He was amiable and winning and attractive, and was loved and respected by the numerous converts that he gained to the

Church. This I know, and could mention amongst his converts some that were devoted friends. But it so happened that amongst the converts there was a small party who were opposed to, rather than led by, their Bishop. A few neophite converts figured as leaders, and the feeling against the Bishop ran so high that it was asserted amongst them that in five days His Lordship would be unmitred, one gentleman undertaking to eat Trajan's pillar if *he* (the Bishop) were not thus degraded; and yet a Bishop, writing to Dr. Baines, said, "Certainly, my Lord, it was high time and necessary that something should be done to stem the torrent of enthusiasm and intemperate zeal that was hurrying us on to serious injury, if not to ruin." Another distinguished Ecclesiastic wrote, "I have read your Pastoral with great pleasure and approbation. I found it well suited to the present time and embracing subjects on which I quite think it is the duty of your Lordship to speak,"—and all this time Bishop Baines was not favoured with the name of a single one of his accusers.

I myself was intimately acquainted with one of the foremost of these, a Lady of high rank, clever, zealous, pious, and amiable, and a benefactress of the Church—one who had gained the ear of Pope Gregory XVI., and had cleverly and with the best of motives poured into his ear *her* views of what she thought was best for the Church in England. She and her party (of whom Bishop Baines complained as interfering with the government of his Diocese) had succeeded, as I have said, in having him summoned to Rome to give an account of his stewardship. On examination, it was found, however, that Bishop Baines had written nothing that required retractation.

It must needs strike the impartial reader that there was something in this proceeding which is contrary to our English ideas of fair play. To be suddenly called away from home and occupations by the highest authorities to answer charges made by unknown accusers is, to say the least, very unusual, and in a controversy between the Laity and their Bishop, who should submit? A Bishop must raise his voice when the interests of the Church require it. He must be "opportune" and he must sometimes "importune." He must often "argue," oftener "entreat," and occasionally he must venture to "reprove." This is his duty as laid down by the Apostle; but the Laity, the highest and the best of them, are exhorted to obey.

The truth is that Bishop Baines had an enlightened mind on religious subjects, a strong sense of duty, and a strong will. His accusers were clever, enthusiastic, and well meaning, and in their zeal took up religious questions by the roots.

A part of the Pastoral which is somewhat ambiguous and objected to by the converts is that in which Bishop Baines speaks of a practice of piety "which the Church tolerates rather than approves of, which good taste cannot defend nor reason easily explain." These words are supposed by the accusers to refer to the doctrine of the

Sacred Heart. That this really was the case has not yet been borne out by logical proof, but has been left to supposition. It is well known, however, that Dr. Baines was not favourable to the practices of the devotion to the Sacred Heart at the commencement of its introduction in England; nor need we be surprised when we remember that the devotion to the Sacred Heart had not as yet been so explicitly approved of by the Church as it is now, and also that Dr. Baines was always most careful to avoid anything that could possibly afford reasonable grounds for controversy to those outside the Church.

Another portion of the Pastoral concerns the prayers said for the conversion of England. He objected to and forbade the recital of these prayers on the grounds that any such conversion was not then within the range of moral possibilities. This opinion was assailed by the new converts as being derogatory to the Divine Mercy, and as disapproving and condemning what the Holy See encouraged and commanded.

But after all the Bishop simply stated what certainly was a fact, namely, that the conversion of England was by no means so imminent as people, in their enthusiasm, imagined; nay, it seemed to be just then, humanly speaking, morally impossible. Nor are we told that the Holy See absolutely commanded and enjoined the use of these prayers, but simply that the Holy See gave an expression of opinion regarding them.

Such questions as the "Immaculate Conception," which had not then been defined as an article of faith, were taken up by these devotees. Whoever will look at Volume I., page 104, of the "Prior Park Theology," published under Bishop Baines' direction, will find that His Lordship was a believer in the doctrine of the Immaculate Conception of the Blessed Virgin Mary as far as anyone can be a believer in a doctrine which is not of *faith.* But because he objected to its being brought forward in the title pages published in a Protestant country, he was accused of denying the doctrine altogether, and of being wanting in respect to the Holy Mother of our Redeemer.

The Decrees of Propaganda of the 29th of December, 1838, alluded to in the Declarations made by Bishop Baines, had reference to the building of Churches in England, the question at issue between the Bishops and Propaganda being whether the "Regulars" were to be permitted to build their Churches without the consent of their Bishops.

Again, the view which Bishop Baines took of the word "Heretic" did not suit his accusers. He did not approve of a Protestant being called a *Heretic* unless he or she remained *obstinate* in error. The Bishop's accusers considered that his views on the subject indicated an undue leaning on his part to his heterodox countrymen, whom he was, they said, disposed to flatter. In the language employed by the Church in her public documents, the word Heretic is employed to designate all who are separable from the Catholic Church by merely holding erroneous tenets, or who belong, however inculpably, to heretical sects. The Douay

Catechism, however, in common use in England defines heresy an *obstinate* error in matters of faith.

There now remains the last part of the Pastoral, in which the Bishop entreats his faithful to pray "for our beloved Queen, that God may crown her with all blessings spiritual and temporal; and as her recent union with the Prince Albert makes her happiness dependent on his, we enjoin," he said, "that the name of His Royal Highness be added to that of Her Majesty in the prayer usually added to the Postcommunion, of which we subjoin a form:—

"Oratio Postcommunioni Addenda.

"Et famulos tuos Gregorium Papam, Petrum antistitem nostrum, Victoriam Reginam nostram, cum Alberto consorte, cum domo regia, cum populo et exercitu ipsi commissis, ab omni adversitate custodi; pacem tuam nostris concede temporibus, et ab Ecclesia tua cunctam repelle nequitiam. Per Dominum," etc.

Dr. Baines, in certain prayers not said at Mass, is accused of omitting any mention regarding the Sovereign Pontiff and the Catholic Church, and of thus limiting his solicitude to obtaining the favour of the Government and the Protestants.

It is perfectly true that no explicit mention is made of the name of the Holy Father in these prayers; but in the Postcommunion given above in Latin, the name of the then reigning Pontiff is put in the first place as one of those to be prayed for. Having, therefore, been implicitly mentioned in the Mass, it was not necessary to mention it again in connection with prayers said for the Queen and Royal Family.

The whole of the proceedings as stated by His Lordship were as follows :—"The Pastoral was denounced at Rome, by whom, I repeat, I know not; a long list of charges was preferred against it—I answered those charges in ample detail. A Select Congregation of Cardinals, comprising some of the most distinguished Members of the Sacred College, was appointed to examine into the case, and the decision was, not that I should retract a word of what I had written, but that I should repel the attack made upon my character by putting forth a disavowal of certain acts and opinions which had been publicly imputed to me. This demand was just and necessary, inasmuch as I could not, as a Bishop, allow my character to be unjustly aspersed. At the same time, as I had never done the acts nor held the opinions imputed to me, I had not the slightest objection to make the declarations required; nor did I hesitate for one single moment to make them. On the contrary, I was glad to have an opportunity of disavowing, in the most public manner, the truth of the charges which, in spite of previous repeated disavowals, certain persons have long obstinately persisted in imputing to me."

Declarations Presented to His Holiness.

"*First*, I engaged publicly to declare, as I now do, that I never intended in any way to allude in the Pastoral to the Decrees of Propaganda of the

29th September, 1838, which Decrees, as explained by Propaganda, I fully receive and consider as the conscientious rule of my conduct. As to ridiculing those who patronise or observe them, I should think it wrong to do so, and certainly never intended to do it.

"*Secondly*, I engaged to declare that in no part of the Pastoral did I mean to disapprove of the devotion to the Sacred Heart as far as it has had the approbation of the Holy See. If I alluded to the subject at all, it was only to disapprove of certain inaccurate expressions contained in books which the Holy See has never approved, or of the imprudent way in which the devotion is sometimes practised or brought forward. As to the doctrine of the Immaculate Conception, all I alluded to in the Pastoral was the making dedications to it of books, which were liable to fall into the hands of Protestants, to whom I considered that such dedications were more likely to give scandal than edification. On these as well as all other doctrines and practices, I do and always have approved whatever the Church or its organ, the Holy See, approves.

"*Thirdly*, I promised to declare that I did not in the Pastoral disapprove *of prayers in general* for the conversion of England, some of which I ordered, much less did I disapprove of any particular prayers which the Holy See had approved; that the only prayers I prohibited in the Pastoral, as expressly stated in my answers to the charges, was a weekly Mass proposed to be celebrated publicly for the immediate national conversion of

England. I have no hesitation, however, in adding that should the Holy See approve or command such Mass, I shall certainly approve and enforce it.

"*Fourthly*, I said the same of pious associations and pious exercises of all kinds. It undoubtedly belongs to the Holy See to sanction such matters by its authority, and it is undoubtedly my duty, as a Bishop and Vicar Apostolic, to obey its regulations.

"*Fifthly*, I have already said, and here again openly declare, that I had no intention of applying the remarks I made in the Pastoral respecting converts, *to the whole body of them in general,* but only to certain individuals, who were animated by a zeal which appeared to me imprudent, and calculated to injure rather than benefit religion. In applying to them certain texts from the Epistles of St. Paul to the Corinthians and Timothy, I never meant to insinuate that those converts were guilty of the same offences as are mentioned by St. Paul, or to impeach in any way either their faith, their morality, or their good intentions.

"In objecting to the term *Heretics* being applied indiscriminately to Protestants, I declared that I did not mean to deny that the term may be applied in a correct theological sense to any sect which denies the Articles of the Catholic Faith, and is separated from the centre of Catholic unity, but only to assert that some individuals, who err invincibly and without obstinacy, are not *Heretics* in the strict and formal sense of the term, and that harsh appellations, however true, ought to be refrained from, as more likely to repel men from the truth than to allure them to it.

"As to the charge of wishing to flatter Protestants, I referred to the passage of the Pastoral in which I compare the Anglican Clergy to the pagan priesthood in proof that such charge is groundless. And as to the complaint that I have seemed to place myself in opposition to the Holy See, I could only regret, if this had happened through any fault of mine, it having ever been my intention, as it was undoubtedly my duty to show every deference, respect, and obedience to that supreme authority.

"I delivered the foregoing Declarations into the hands of His Holiness on the 16th March, and never shall I forget the kind, benevolent, and paternal tenderness which he expressed on the occasion. He promised that he would write me a letter, which I might show in self-defence, and that he would also write to all the English Vicars Apostolic to inform them of the happy termination of this unpleasant affair. When I took my leave, he loaded me with benedictions. On the 19th, His Holiness again sent for me, and read the letter he had written to me, the extreme kindness of which I immediately saw, and for which I returned him my ardent thanks.

"As I was well aware that there were persons who would feel disappointed at the result of this affair, and who would be tempted to put forth accounts more conformable to their wishes than to 'matter of fact,' I requested that His Holiness would give me his sanction for publishing a new edition of the Pastoral, with the substance of the Declarations I had presented to him appended, to which he graciously assented, adding, 'Take notice that you have not been required to retract anything.' At the same time, he expressed his earnest wish that whatsoever was calculated to excite angry feelings should be avoided as much as possible, which I promised him should be done, as far as I was concerned. His Holiness then presented me with a thousand crowns in gold, to defray the expenses of my journey, and again loaded me with the kindest caresses and the most fervent benedictions.

"The following is a literal translation of His Holiness's letter, written with his own hand, and delivered by him on that occasion into mine:—

"'To Our Venerable Brother, PETER AUGUSTINE BAINES, Bishop of Siga and Vicar Apostolic in the Western District of England.

"'Venerable Brother,—

"'The injunction, Venerable Brother, which with paternal charity we addressed to you in our letter of the 16th of January of the current year, and with which your docility, religion, and deference to the Holy See caused us to anticipate your compliance, we exceedingly rejoice in the Lord, and cordially congratulate with you that you have faithfully fulfilled. For the written Declarations of the 15th instant, which you delivered to us in person, respecting the Pastoral put forth by you on the 24th of February of the past year, satisfies, we find, both the decision of the Select Congregation and our own exhortations, and therefore we most willingly admit it, not doubting that what you promise you will seasonably fulfil.

" 'Go on, therefore, Venerable Brother, to preserve the bond of sacerdotal concord and the unity of spirit with your colleagues, the Vicars Apostolic and other Pastors of Souls; and remember the saying of St. Leo, "That it is our duty and yours to establish, by the grace of charity, what by no insidious art of the Devil may be overthrown." In the meantime, whilst we embrace you with fatherly affection, we most affectionately impart to you our Apostolical Benediction.

" 'Given in Rome, at St. Peter's, the 19th of March, 1841.

GREGORY P.P. XVI.'

" On the 27th of the same month, I left Rome for England, where I found that certain very erroneous and injurious statements respecting these events, proceeding from persons of great respectability, had arrived before me, and rendered indispensable this simple narrative of facts. May it be productive of the peace I so earnestly desire!"

Extracts from a LETTER of the RIGHT HONOURABLE LORD CLIFFORD, dated Rome, June 5th, 1841, addressed to the RIGHT REVEREND DR. BAINES, Vicar Apostolic of the Western District.

" By the words which the Holy Father then repeated to me, in the presence of Mr. and Mrs.

H. Weld, their daughter Appolonia, and my son Henry, who can all, as well as myself, swear to the fact, His Holiness declared to me that *it was impossible to call upon you to retract any expression in your Lenten Pastoral of last year, because retractation could only be required where manifest error existed, and your Pastoral was not, in his opinion, liable to any such imputation.*"

"His Holiness would never allow me, in speaking of the *Declarations* he might require or had required from your Lordship, to make use of the word *retractation*, or even *explanation*, in reference to what he required of your Lordship."

In conclusion, Bishop Baines, though of humble origin, was a great man, and was in advance of the age in which he lived. He was plunged, as it were, in a rapid stream where various currents met, and he had to stem them as best he could. He was, moreover, at the head of the Vicars Apostolic, and led the way in those troublesome times, and had mainly to bear the brunt for all. Bishop Briggs, who delivered the funeral oration of Bishop Baines, amongst other things, said:— "The Pastorals which he addressed to his district —and not to *his* district alone, but to the Catholics of all England, who looked to him with the highest interest for instruction—were eagerly read and severely criticised. Upon some of his Pastorals there was a difference of opinion, and it would be unbecoming to discuss them now. But yet it is in the presence of that Omnipotent Being, before Whom I am soon to be answerable for what I say, that I speak of him, who is now no more, and whose most intimate friendship I enjoyed. I hesitate not to say that, whether he were mistaken or not mistaken in those addresses, he had no other view in them than the glory of God, the propagation of his truth, and the cause of our most holy faith; and that he never wished to wound the feelings of any member of the household of the faith."

CHAPTER IV.

The Death of Dr. Baines.

BISHOP BAINES, being now left to the resources of his own Diocese, called in such Ecclesiastics as he considered would be most useful to him, and most suited to the wants of the College, under altered circumstances.

In the Very Reverend Monsignor Thomas Brindle he had, from first to last, a constant friend. The Rev. Dr. Rooker, Monsignor Bonomi, Canon Shattock, and the Rev. James Baines were staunch adherents of the Bishop.

At St. Peter's College, the Rev. Jacob Illingworth (after having been Prefect for many years) became President. His old friend and colleague, Mr. James Cavanagh, worked disinterestedly with him, and for many long years both may be said to have "borne the burthen and heat of the day." With these and other young teachers—lay and clerical—a new era commenced.

The Bishop's nephew, the Rev. James Baines, had been absent from the College for two years, in the capacity of tutor to the young Earl of Shrewsbury. He travelled with him on the continent, and tarried some time in Rome. Having much of his uncle's good taste for architecture, he took advantage of his opportunities, and paid great attention to the subject, which he afterwards turned to good account for the benefit of the College. When a boy, untutored in the art, he had made an architectural drawing of the façade of Prior Park, which Dr. Baines took to Rome for the inspection of Pope Leo XII.

Being in urgent need of his assistance, the Bishop recalled him to Prior Park, and made him Procurator, with the general management of the temporalities of the College. In his new office, the Procurator made many improvements; but it was evident that the *means* necessary for paying his way were wanting.

The fire which destroyed the mansion (and of which I shall have more to say hereafter) was financially ruinous—a loss of £15,000 being only partially covered by an insurance of two or three thousand pounds. Dr. Baines had expended about £50,000 on buildings and embellishments; and no wonder that the resources of the Bishop and his Procurator were well-nigh exhausted. The failing condition of the great work of His Lordship's life seemed to tell seriously upon his health. Ever zealous in the discharge of his episcopal functions, he preached the opening sermon of St. Mary's on the Quay, at Bristol.

A remarkable incident occurred on the eve of Bishop Baines' death. On his return home from Bristol, instead of joining the dinner party, he withdrew for a while to his room. During the dessert, he came into the hall for about twenty minutes. Amongst the guests was one who had sung an old College song, at the close of which the Bishop reminded him that he had left out one of the verses. This the Bishop then sang himself The words were the following :—

"Ubi sunt qui ante nos
In mundo fuere?
Abeas ad inferos,
Transeas ad superos
Hos si vis videre."

Translation.

"Those who lived before us, where are they now?
If you wish again to see them,
Amidst God's Angels you must seek them,
Or find them in the realms below."

Within an hour or two after the Bishop had sung these words in the Latin version, death had quietly come to him in his sleep.

I had occasion to speak with His Lordship on his return from Bristol, and to my inquiries as to how he felt after his exertions, he replied in a sad tone, "I do not know, Mr. Shepherd." The next morning, July 6th, 1843, the Bishop was found dead in bed.

The following letter from Mr. Edward King, solicitor, of 13, Queen Square, Bath, to Mr. Lucas, editor of the *Tablet*, gives us an authentic account of Dr. Baines' death :—

"Bath, July 6th, 1843.

"My dear Sir,—

"We are in sad affliction here. It has pleased Almighty God, in His all-wise disposition, to take from us our dearly-beloved Bishop, who died at an early hour this morning. I have, at the request of Dr. Brindle, undertaken to give you the circumstances attendant on this sad event.

"Tuesday was the day of the annual exhibition

of studies at the College, at which the Bishop assisted, and afterwards distributed the prizes. The following day (yesterday) was appointed for the solemn dedication of the new Catholic Church of St. Mary's, at Bristol, at which the Bishop assisted, and preached a most powerful sermon on the marks of the true Church. Nearly forty of the Clergy were present. A very considerable number accompanied him back to Bath, and dined at Prior Park. His Lordship did not appear to be more fatigued than would have been expected. He did not, however, join the dinner table, but went to lie down. In the course of the evening, he came into the hall and sat about twenty minutes, apparently much refreshed; but he admitted he had not eaten anything. The company retired about nine o'clock, after which the Bishop went to his room, took a little cold chicken and wine, and went to rest about ten, saying to his servant he felt better. Alas! during this night was our dear and beloved father taken from us. Soon after six in the morning, he was found in bed insensible, and it was thought he had fainted. Dr. Brindle was immediately summoned, and administered the last Sacrament, with the hopes that life was not quite extinct. He could not have suffered much, as his bell was immediately at hand, and the clothes of the bed were undisturbed. Thus, in the immediate exercise of his high functions, and, as it may be said, in the arms of the Clergy (for many slept in the College that night), was called out of this world the Right Reverend Dr. Baines, Bishop of Siga and V.A.

of the Western District. It is not a little remarkable that the event took place on the octave-day of the feast of SS. Peter and Paul, and of his patron Saint.

"The Holy Sacrifice was immediately offered up by the numerous Priests in the College.

"I send you this information that you may be able to announce the event to the Catholic world, and which you will please to do in your own way and words.

"Believe me, Sir, yours truly,

"EDWARD KING.

"F. Lucas, Esq."

Dr. Baines' health was generally delicate; he had felt a peculiar sensation of numbness for years, which brought on a paralytic affection about two years previous to his death. At the inquest held by Mr. Alban English, solicitor, of Bath—the City Coroner—Mr. Church, His Lordship's medical attendant, deposed :—

"I have attended the Bishop professionally for some time. About two years ago, I was called in to attend him for paralytic affection, from which he soon recovered. Upon that occasion, he lost his speech, and also the use of his arm and leg. Since then, I have been in daily attendance upon him when at home. He has never had any serious illness since that time. I saw him for the last time alive on Monday, previous to his going to Bristol; he complained of no pain whatever in his head, though he said he was not well. I think an unusual exertion likely to have been attended with danger to his life, and have advised him to keep himself more quiet; and he has expressed his sorrow that he was obliged to exert himself so much. I saw him this morning about seven o'clock, when he appeared to have been dead about three or four hours. I think the cause of his death was apoplexy, united with his previous attack. On Monday, he seemed in his usual health, except that he complained a little more. I never entertained an idea of his dying so suddenly; he has been keeping himself more quiet of late in accordance with my advice."

His death seemed to be the departure of the master spirit which had originated, guided, and fostered the College for so many years; and nothing could equal the grief and dismay which was felt, not only at Prior Park, but in Bath, and, indeed, throughout the whole district.

The time of the funeral had at first been talked of for an earlier day; but it was at length fixed for Thursday, the 13th, and at the earnest request of the most respectable Protestant inhabitants, it was determined that the corpse should lie in state on the Tuesday and Wednesday previous, to allow His Lordship's numerous admirers and friends to pay a last tribute of respect to his memory. Accordingly, on those two days, between the hours of eleven and six, the great hall at the Mansion House was thrown open to the public, who were admitted in parties of a hundred or a hundred and fifty at a time, and allowed to contemplate for a moment the sad spectacle, and then to pass out at another door. The entrance door was attended by four policemen, whose services were hardly ever more needed than on the latter of the two days. On Tuesday, the crowd was not trifling, upwards of three thousand persons having been present. But on Wednesday, when the fact of the lying in state was more generally known, the number of visitors was more than tripled. It is calculated that nearly ten thousand persons passed through the hall on Wednesday. The crowding at the entrance was excessive. Fashionably-dressed ladies struggled for admission with the utmost earnestness, and with the most perfect indifference, not only as to their dresses, but even as to the safety of their persons; and when, at length, the doors were finally closed, they shut out at least two or three thousand disappointed visitors, some of whom had come from as far as Nottingham, and who remained for hours, continuing still to hope for admission.

On Thursday morning, at nine o'clock, the Office for the Dead commenced. Matins and Lauds were chanted in the great hall, which presented the same appearance that it had done during the two previous days. Under a canopy was laid the coffin, upon which, on a brass plate in the shape of a mitre, was the following inscription :—

PETRUS AUGUSTINUS BAINES,
EPISCOPUS SIGENSIS, V.A.D.O.
OBIIT ANNO DOMINI MDCCCXLIII.
PRID. NON. JULII. VIXIT AN. LVII. DIES XII.

Upon the coffin was laid an episcopal crook, mitre, and hat, a chalice, paten, and ciborium. Around at the corners of the coffin, the episcopal vestments were tastefully arranged. At the head was the Bishop's throne, about which were disposed another mitre, processional cross, vestments, etc., etc.

The office was performed in private. There were present four bishops—Dr. Griffiths, Dr. Briggs, Dr. Gillies, and Dr. Morris—and about forty priests.

Now about the same time, it also pleased God to remove Dr. Baines' nephew from his sphere of usefulness. He was a young man of great physical power, and unequalled in the games and sports at the College; and his death from typhus fever, after a very short illness, took his friends quite by surprise. His loss at the College was great; for being co-trustee with Dr. Brindle and Canon Shattock, he naturally took a great interest in everything that concerned Prior Park. The present generation is indebted to him for great improvements in the farm buildings near St. Paul's. He also gave directions for the plans of the new Church, and superintended the building until the walls had reached to half their intended elevation. If, however, I were to leave an impression on the minds of my readers that the new Church owes its origin either to Bishop Baines or his nephew, I should do an injustice to the memory of a great benefactress to Prior Park—good Miss Bettington, who resided at Devonshire Buildings, Bath. She gave two thousand pounds to initiate the work; and this she did at the request, and out of regard for the Reverend Charles (afterwards the Right Reverend Monsignor) Parfitt.

It now only remains to be said, in reference to Bishop Baines and his nephew, that they were called from their labours when they were both comparatively young and vigorous, the former being 57 years of age and the latter 32. They were buried at Prior Park; but when the property passed from Ecclesiastical hands, the English Benedictine fathers, in a kindly spirit, translated their remains to the cemetery of Downside College, where they now rest, and "may they rest in peace."

CHAPTER V.

THE COLLAPSE OF OLD PRIOR PARK.

AFTER some unavoidable delay Bishop Baggs, the successor of Dr. Baines, arrived at Prior Park with two Ecclesiastics—Dr. Fergusson and Don Castro Gonzalas—and a professor of music—Signor Ravalli.

Before proceeding further, I will briefly sketch the ecclesiastical career of Bishop Baggs.

Bishop Baggs (Charles Michael) was an eminent controversialist, scholar, and antiquary, and illustrious by his family connections.

He commenced his ecclesiastical studies in the year 1821, at St. Edmund's College, in Herefordshire. For four years he continued his studies there with intense application, and was remarkable for his docility and intelligence. In the spring of 1825 he was sent to the English College in Rome, which for fifteen years became his home. His remarkable ability was shown in a signal manner on the 25th of September, 1830, when, in the presence of a distinguished audience presided over by Cardinal Zurla, he held his ground as a Latin disputant, against all comers, in the maintenance of an unusually ample thesis as a theologian. They embraced 50 in regard to Holy Writ, 41 in regard to Dogmatic Theology, and 60 in regard to Ecclesiastical History. This display won for him his Doctor's Cap, at the early age of 24.

He was ordained priest in his 25th year, and took high rank in the English College as a teacher. For several years he occupied the Chair of Professor of Hebrew. His knowledge of French, Italian, German, and Spanish was remarkable. As a pulpit orator, he could not be classed with his predecessor, Bishop Baines, though he wrote and preached and published many discourses, notably on the Supremacy of the Roman Pontiffs, in the Church of Gesú e Maria, in the Corso, Feb. 7th, 1836.

On Dec. 23rd, 1840, Monsignor Baggs was selected, by reason of his near relationship, to preach the funeral oration of his cousin, Gwendoline Talbot, Princess Borghese. The affecting sermon was inscribed to her father, the 16th Earl of Shrewsbury.

Throughout the Pontificate of Gregory XVI., Monsignor Baggs was the Camerière d'onore upon whom devolved the duty of presenting all the English visitors to His Holiness. In this capacity he enjoyed a high degree of popularity. His career at Rome was fittingly closed by his elevation to the episcopacy, to fill the suddenly vacated office of Vicar Apostolic of the Western District in England, in consequence of the death of Bishop Baines. With such prestige, and with such a reputation for learning, no wonder that His Lordship was heartily welcomed by his Clergy and by the Laity of the Western District. And not only was he remarkable for vigorous capacity and learning, but his dominant characteristics were extreme amiability and gentleness, so much so that he was popularly spoken of by those under his jurisdiction and care as "Pacificus."

His Lordship took possession of his Diocese in due form, and on the 30th of May, 1844, the ceremony of installation took place in the Mansion Chapel. The new Bishop took up his permanent abode at the College, and seemed to be delighted with everything he saw. Ascending the magnificent flight of steps leading to the portico, and viewing the splendid mansion, he observed in his humorous style, "Si sta comomdo qui"—"One may be very comfortable here." He commenced his episcopacy by studying the best interests of his College and Diocese. He established conferences at Prior Park, which were well attended by the Clergy, and at which he himself presided. He gave a week's Retreat personally to the whole house, and, according to the judgment of competent persons, was remarkable for his logical and close reasoning. In due time, he made the visitation of his Diocese, and preached and gave a Retreat to the nuns at Stape Hill. It was my privilege to accompany and assist His Lordship on this occasion.

Not less attentive to the wants of the College, the new Bishop appointed Superiors and Teachers, and gave such directions as he considered good for the advancement of the best interests of the establishment. Monsignor Thomas Brindle was appointed President of St. Paul's, and Monsignor Parfitt of St. Peter's.

I can remember being somewhat surprised at seeing Monsignor Brindle presiding in the refectory at St. Paul's (there were two refectories and two kitchens at Prior Park, each College having its own culinary staff), because up to this period Monsignor Brindle had not taken any active part in teaching or in presiding over the students. He did not continue long in this office, but was succeeded by the Reverend William Vaughan (afterwards Bishop of Plymouth). During the summer of 1845, Monsignor Parfitt was a practical Superior and an efficient Teacher at St. Peter's. Both Colleges were well filled, and the studies were well conducted; but however excellent the views of Bishop Baggs may have been concerning the government of his Diocese and the College, they were prematurely interrupted by his death, on the 16th of October, 1845. His Lordship's death was announced in the *Tablet* in the following words:—

"It has pleased Almighty God to cast us once more in deep affliction, by taking from us our esteemed and revered Bishop. Tuesday last, about 2 o'clock p.m., His Lordship was seized with an affection in the throat, which caused us great alarm; he then rallied and seemed to recover his spirits. The attack, however, returned about 2 on Wednesday afternoon. His medical attendants, who were with him a great part of the evening, feared the worst; and soon after 2 o'clock on Thursday morning he expired, invoking the intercession of the Mother of God. His Lordship, who was sensible to the last, was strengthened in his last conflict by all the rites of our Holy Religion, Oct. 18th, 1845."

There was now an interregnum, which lasted until the arrival of Bishop Ullathorne, in the summer of 1846. His Lordship was consecrated at Coventry on the 21st of June, 1846, and arrived at Prior Park at the end of June in the same year. During this interregnum, the Rev. Monsignor Brindle and the Rev. Thomas Shattock, from their long residence at the College and from the fact of their being the Trustees of the Estate, became, in the natural order of things, the acknowledged Superiors in the absence of a Bishop.

Dr. Vaughan and Monsignor Parfitt had every possible assistance and support in conducting the classes, by the accession of several distinguished and learned converts, who seemed wishful to make Prior Park their home, and to work together for its benefit. Foremost amongst these was Mr. Capes, a converted Protestant clergyman, from Bridgewater, who taught mathematics and music for some time; an Italian, Canon Rossi, filled the Theological Chair. Mr. Charles Henry Collins, who was received into the Church, at Prior Park, on All Saints' Day, 1845, taught at the College until August, 1846. At this period, William Clifford, afterwards Bishop Clifford, was the Prefect at St. Paul's College. Before joining the Redemptorists, the late Bishop of Southwark, Dr. Coffin, was one of the Professors at Prior Park. He arrived at the College in company with Cardinal Newman, and was received into the Church by Dr. Brindle. The ceremony took place in the Bishop's Chapel, in the Mansion. Herbert Woollett, afterwards Vicar General of the Plymouth Diocese, was also a Professor at Prior Park at this time.

In August, 1848, owing to some disagreement with the Regent (Monsignor Brindle), nine Superiors and Professors tendered their resignation to him on the same day and at the same hour, the President of St. Paul's (Dr. Vaughan) leading the way and the President of St. Peter's (Dr. Parfitt) bringing up the rear. It is not within my province to enter into the cause of this untoward event, and yet, without some words of explanation, it would seem almost incredible. It took place during a period of interregnum, when there was no master mind to conciliate, guide, and utilise this large and intelligent staff of Professors. The head of the College was not a practical Superior, and had never taught, in any capacity, from the foundation of the College. Under these circumstances, it could scarcely be expected that there should exist, on the part of the Professors, that confidence in their leader which in all undertakings is an element of success. It was felt, therefore, to be necessary that the Regent should resign his office, and place the reins of government in more experienced hands. This was notified to him, and he was given to understand that unless he did resign, they were prepared to leave the College *en masse*, and at once. The Regent, having sunk a large sum of money in the College, resolved not to resign, and the sad result of his resolve is too well known. Another explanation of the resignation of the Professors is that they wished to protest against the refusal of the Trustees to hand over the *property in the establishment* to the new Bishop. Dr. Ullathorne thereupon declined to have anything more to do with the place, but gave permission to Dr. Brindle to carry it on, if he could procure Professors for the purpose. Probably both these explanations are closely connected, and merely require to be combined and adjusted.

Dr. Ullathorne's first appearance in the Diocese in the discharge of his episcopal functions was when, on the feast of "St. Peter in Chains," August 7th, 1846, he sang the Vespers in the Bishop's Chapel, in the Mansion. He soon left the College, the future success of which he seems to have regarded as quite problematical.

About this time, I was not strong in health, and had obtained leave of absence. I had been at Prior Park fifteen years, and wished for a change; accordingly I petitioned the new Bishop to be allowed to remain in the Lancashire Diocese among my friends. Bishop Ullathorne yielded to my urgent request, and in a very kind letter, dated March 23rd, 1847, notified his acceptance of the resignation, adding, "I have had a good testimony of you for the time you have been in the district, and I really feel an interest in you, and I regret to part with you without having the consolation of ever having seen you."

The statements which I have to make for the next period must necessarily be from information received from others. I will endeavour to be as exact as possible under the circumstances, and will, at least, make my readers acquainted with the most important facts connected with the closing of the College on January 1st, 1856.

From notes supplied to me from Bishop Clifford, I am able to state that Bishop Ullathorne was succeeded by Bishop Hendren, who was appointed Vicar Apostolic of the Western District by a Brief dated July 30th, 1848. At the division of the Western District into Dioceses in September, 1850, Dr. Hendren became Bishop of Clifton, and remained so until June, 1851. He did not reside at Prior Park, and presumably did not take any special interest in the College.

Dr. Hendren was succeeded by Dr. Burgess, who was consecrated on the 27th of July, 1851. It will be remembered that he had been the Prior of Ampleforth, and that, influenced by Dr. Baines, he resigned his office and left the Benedictine Order, to assist Dr. Baines in the establishment of Prior Park. We may naturally suppose, then, that he had the interests of the College much at heart. Moreover, he was the bosom friend of the Regent of the College, and of Dr. Rooker, who was devoting himself, heart and soul, to the improvement of those who were under his care. Canon Shattock, too, was linked in closest friendship with all three, and was co-trustee of the Prior Park Estate with the Regent. Notwithstanding the abrupt resignation of so many excellent Professors, there were still some able men left. There was Mr. James Cavanagh, ever faithful to the powers that were, and constant in the discharge of his duties ; there was the Rev. Brande Morris, not to mention other efficient teachers.

And that they *were* efficient and successful may be surmised from the "fruits" and results of their united efforts. To those efforts, for instance, are to be attributed the development of the talents of many boys, who have since occupied useful and distinguished positions in the world. Among these were Monsignor Edward Williams, D.D., Monsignor James Williams, and Major-General William Graham, Señor Guibara, and others. "By their fruits you shall know them."

Bishop Burgess did not reside at the College; but it cannot be doubted that he did all in his power to sustain it, under overwhelming difficulties. He personally collected money to supply immediate wants; but the sums subscribed were wholly inadequate to the necessities of the case. Dr. Burgess died November 27th, 1854. His successor, Bishop Clifford, was not consecrated until February 15th, 1857; hence there was an interregnum of more than two years, during which time Archbishop Errington was Administrator of the Diocese.

In the meantime, tradespeople were clamorous for their money, and the annual payment of £900 (interest on a mortgage of £18,000) was a call to which those who had the management of the finances could not respond. The mortgagee, who, by the terms of his mortgage, stood in the position of landlord, was Mr. Edward Raphael, the nephew of Mr. Alexander Raphael, who had originally lent the money. The interest not being forthcoming, Mr. Edward Raphael took possession of the Prior Park Estate, and distrained for his interest as for rent.

Archbishop Errington, in his Pastoral Letter issued on the subject at Prior Park, on the 31st of January, 1856, says:—"On the first day of the year, legal proceedings were taken by the landlord. The property still remaining on the premises was valued, and estimated as more than equal to outstanding claims; to satisfy which, in the first instance, it was being sold." The execution here alluded to was put in on January 1st, 1856. Everything was sold by public auction. From the time of this execution to the restoration on the 23rd April, 1867, eleven years and nearly four months intervened. The disastrous fire which wrecked the Mansion in the month of May, 1836, had much to do with the closing of the College. It occurred before the death of Bishop Baines, and he lived to see the building restored. An account of what took place during the conflagration, and also of the rebuilding of the Mansion, will be given in Part the Second.

In a history of this kind, embracing as it does more than sixty years, with a break of eleven years, consecutive chapters, in reference to time, cannot well be given. Facts seem to be connected with each other and live on through long periods of time, and provided those facts are truthfully given and with accurate dates, their *exact* position in the history is not of much importance. The author trusts, therefore, that the reader's kind indulgence may be extended to him should the order of dates in any respect appear inverted.

PART II.

CHAPTER I.

The Building of the Mansion.

HAVING now traced the history of the College, I will append some remarks as to the buildings themselves, and give some information, which I have hitherto omitted lest I should unduly interrupt the thread of my narrative.

As I have casually mentioned, Prior Park owes its origin to Ralph Allen. This prominent citizen of Bath was born at St. Blazey, near St. Austel, in Cornwall, A.D. 1693. The place of his birth was an inn, called "The Duke William," about a mile and a half on the high road to the town. In those days, it was a renowned establishment, and, though changed into a farm-house, is still pointed out, with respect, as the birthplace of Ralph Allen. Bishop Warburton, who resided for some time at Prior Park, would not allow the real founder of Prior Park to be styled the "low-born," but the "humble" Allen.

It is recorded that young Allen was employed, by his grandmother, in the management of the Post Office at St. Colomb, in Cornwall. In this capacity, he soon attracted the attention of the Post Office Inspector, who, being highly pleased with the neatness and accuracy of young Allen's figures and accounts, expressed a wish to see the boy in a situation where his ingenuity and industry might have a wider scope. That situation was in the Post Office in Bath. In the year 1715, at the age of twenty-two, Allen was still one of the clerks in the Bath Post Office; but at that period he was promoted, at the instance of General Wade, to the responsible position of Postmaster. This promotion is believed to have been due to the discovery by Allen of a Jacobite rising in the West of England. Admiring the young man's character and ability, the Commander shortly afterwards married him to Miss Earl, his daughter. Allen's progress in civic standing and consideration must have been rapid, for we find him in 1722, on the evidence of a picture of him lately discovered, a member of the Common Council. His influence was supreme in the Corporation and out of it, and his services were so eminent, and his conduct so prudent, that he never for a moment ceased to possess the absolute confidence of the whole city. In 1742 he was Mayor of Bath.

In his situation of Postmaster, Ralph Allen devised and successfully carried out the system of Cross Posts, which revolutionised the whole Post Office organisation. By these "Cross Posts," he connected the West of England with the Lancashire District and the mail route to Ireland; giving at the same time independent postal inter-communication to all the important towns lying in the direction to be taken. Previous to this change, letters passing between neighbouring towns were conveyed by strangely circuitous routes; for instance, letters passing from Cheltenham or Bath to Worcester or Birmingham had to go first to London, and then be forwarded to their destination by another postal road. Ralph Allen undertook to add £6,000 a year to the revenue. His success was so great that at a later period he was glad to pay the Government £20,000 a year for the privilege of carrying on the enterprise. Even at that price, the contract brought him in, on an average, £12,000 a year. When we take into consideration that Mr. Allen's improvements were carried on exclusively by bridle horses, we may well imagine the inconvenience which was caused by the delay of letters. The "good old times" in which our forefathers lived furnished a fruitful field for Allen's observation, clear intellect, and genius, for the organisation of his postal system. Mr. Allen dealt also largely in the stone business, and was the owner of the quarries on Combe Down and of the Prior Park Estate. The road down from Prior Park to Bath was a tram-road, connecting the works on Combe Down with the river Avon, the wharf being on the Quay in the Strand, in Claverton Street. The Avon had been rendered navigable to Bristol, and by means of this river communication, Allen developed the stone quarrying business to a very great extent. Moreover, with the invaluable assistance of Mr. Wood—the architect of the beautiful Crescents and Squares, the Circus, and other buildings in Bath—Mr. Allen conducted a business of great magnitude, supplying all the stone for the great architect's contracts for the building of modern Bath. Allen wished to introduce his stone into the London market, but met with great opposition. Architects and builders compared his stone to Cheshire cheese, not only in colour and texture, but even in liability to breed maggots, which would soon devour it. They said it would not bear any weight, and was wholly unfit for London work. To prove to the world that all this was mere prejudice, and that the Bath stone was well suited for building purposes, he resolved to exhibit it in a mansion, near his works, to greater advantage than it had ever appeared before. When the palatial edifice of Prior Park was built, the fame of Bath stone spread everywhere, and contracts were sought for public and private buildings.

Ralph Allen had purchased that part of the Priory lands which was called Camalodunum—Combe Down—and it was just under the brow of the hill, at the head of the Combe, that he resolved to build his great mansion. At the period to which I am referring, the site rose somewhat abruptly, and the land was full of water. It was, therefore, necessary to take a wide sweep from the east side, and to level it into the grand terrace-like form to the west which gives it its dignified aspect. Many natural difficulties had to be overcome before the foundations could be laid. Some idea may be formed of the nature of the preparatory work from the fact that 30,000 tons of large blocks of freestone were required for the foundation walls. These foundations, laid in 1735, were for the Mansion in the centre and for two pavilions with wings of offices.

It was fortunate for St. Paul's College that Mr. Allen provided such excellent accommodation for his horses. He is said to have treated them like gentlemen. They were richly caparisoned, and he always had four to his coach and drove out with much state.

The west wing was finished in 1737. After the completion of this wing, the pavilion (where now exists the grand flight of steps leading to the theatre) served as an arch for coaches to drive under.

The Mansion was constructed of solid wrought freestone blocks of very large dimensions, in equal courses, both within and without, so that the walls are equally strong on both sides, and are able to support the incumbent work without being liable to "buckle" under the weight. It should be added that not only are the walls of the entire house, outside and inside, built of Bath stone of the best quality, carefully wrought in the sheds—every stone for its place—but the floors of the basement rooms are laid with the hard, calcined, shelly ragstone which forms, as it were, the roof of the subterranean quarries of softer and less durable stone. The several rooms and passages are vaulted over with stone, so that all the defects peculiar to plaster are effectually avoided in this uniquely constructed house.

Mr. Allen was generous and sympathetic, and the proof of this lies in the interest which he took in the erection of the Bath Mineral Water Hospital. For the building of this, he not only presented the stone, but was a benefactor in many other ways. Personally, Mr. Ralph Allen was about middle height, with handsome mouth, firmly set, and this gave him rather a severe expression, but evidenced nothing more than the firmness and earnestness of his character. His ordinary dress was the brown "cutaway" coat of the period, long waistcoat with large pockets covered with braided flaps, white cambric neckerchief, fine leather "tights," silk stockings, and shoes. For dress, substitute velvet for cloth and black silk for leather.

Prior Park at Allen's death ceased to be what it had been. The society could no longer be kept up. It came into the hands of Bishop Warburton, whose wife was the second Mrs. Allen's niece; and at his death, in 1799, it became the residence of the first Viscount Hawarden, who died without issue in 1807. This nobleman had been connected by marriage with the Allen family; but with his death all direct connection of Prior Park with the Allen family came to an end. From the year 1817, the domain and Mansion, during the occupancy of a Mr. Thomas, suffered much from parsimonious neglect; and a fine avenue of valuable trees in the present playground was cut down with the object of turning the timber into money. A Quaker family named Thomas were the owners of the Estate at the time of the purchase by Dr. Baines.

CHAPTER II.

The Building of St. Paul's College and the Church.

WHEN Bishop Baines had purchased Prior Park, he found himself in possession of a splendid mansion, picturesque and palatial, and so situated as to secure to its owner those blessings of health and cheerfulness, which are to be derived from pure air and the enjoyment of what is beautiful in nature. With all its charming surroundings, however, it was but a mansion, with its stables and farm buildings on one side and its offices on the other—buildings of no mean pretensions, it is true, since they were in keeping with the mansion. Viewing the Colleges of SS. Peter and Paul, as they now stand, critics of to-day may perhaps discover some points therein for animadversion; but had they been confronted, as Dr. Baines was, with stables and the like, and had they been requested to transform them into buildings suitable for colleges, would they have succeeded as well as he in carrying out the work as it now stands?

Dr. Baines, in commencing his work, thought it expedient to utilise as much as possible whatever of the fabric already existed, and, as the walls of the stables were very substantially built, he resolved to erect the College of St. Paul's on the original foundation, leaving the basement intact. Hence we find that the class-rooms at St. Paul's are only a modification of the stables and cow-houses, but so admirably adapted, and so handsome in their proportions, that it is impossible to trace in them the humble purposes to which they were formerly put. Above the stone vaulted ceilings were other compartments of a similar character, but much smaller, built to serve as hay-lofts, granaries, etc. The arched stone roofs were taken down and removed to St. Peter's, to take part in the formation of the class-rooms there. The walls of the stables on which the structure of St. Paul's was erected, were too plain to suit the highly cultured taste of Dr. Baines. He therefore conceived the ingenious plan of cutting the smooth surface into apparently solid blocks of stone. Scaffolds were accordingly erected, and for several weeks the masons were seen, chisel and mallet in hand, transforming the façade of St. Paul's, and giving to it its present substantial and ornamental appearance, as though the lower part of the building had been originally constructed with massive stones. If examined, however, the junction of the stones will not be found where it might be expected, viz., in the indentations made by the chisel and mallet.

The long narrow rooms to the north now used as study and play-rooms, for a long time served as a chapel. At the east end was the sanctuary, the episcopal throne, and the choir for the students —about fifty of whom always came attired in cassock, surplice, and biretta-looking like Church students, and, by their great spirit of piety, rendering the well-conducted services very edifying. The length of the room was broken by the introduction of a pulpit and two light gates of open work, which divided the long room into almost equal parts, the larger portion being set aside for the congregation. During the sermon the gates were thrown open, that the people might the better see and hear the preacher. At the end of the long room was the organ with the lay-choir. Mr. Henry Field took a great interest in the Church music and sang in the choir as a tenor. Under his guidance and that of Mr. Priest, the organist, the Masses of Mozart and Haydn were well rendered by the students, sometimes with the addition of orchestral accompaniments from Bath.

On the ground now occupied by the sanctuary of the new church was a well-built and commodious coach-house, which was converted into an excellent billiard-room. Attached to this was a neat cottage, tenanted by Sergeant Jenkins, who taught fencing and drilling. In 1844 these buildings were taken down to give place to the foundations of the new Church. As has already been stated, the College is indebted to Miss Bettington for the means required for laying these foundations, viz., the sum of two thousand pounds. The ceremony of laying the foundation-stone was performed by Bishop Baggs, in 1844.

The next helping hand was that of the Very Reverend Thomas M. McDonnell. How he came to proffer assistance will require a little explanation. In the Catholic Directory of 1844 the name of the Rev. T. M. McDonnell appears as resident priest at Tor Abbey, Torquay. About this period of his missionary life he received into the Church a young gentleman whose name, unfortunately, seems to be to memory lost. He had come to Torquay in the last stage of consumption. It appears that he was possessed of about £9,000, and had no near relatives to whom he wished to bequeath it. He, therefore, made a will in which he left his money to the Western District for the building of churches. Before the will was returned by the solicitor (Mr. McDonnell, brother of the Canon, to whom it had been forwarded for inspection,) the young man died, and when the will came to hand it was pronounced to be loosely drafted. The informality was discovered by the relatives, who gave notice that they intended to dispute the will. Mr. Edward King, solicitor, of Bath—the legal adviser of Dr. Baines—recommended a compromise, and Canon McDonnell, in the name of the Bishop of the Western District, received £2,000, to be disposed of for the building of churches according to the best of his judgment; and he ultimately came to the conclusion that £1,000 would be well spent in furthering the construction of the new Church at Prior Park. Thus with the £3,000 acquired, the outside walls reached the requisite elevation; but for twenty-seven years no advances towards completion were made. In the year 1867, the College was re-established by Bishop Clifford (some kind friend giving him £4,000), under the presidency of the Right Rev. Monsignor Williams, and four years later the building of the Church was proceeded with. This was owing to a donation of £1,000 from the Duchess of Leeds, and of £500 from Thomas Eyre, Esq., who was educated at Prior Park, with his brother William, now the Rev. Father Eyre, S.J. These donations enabled the Bishop to complete the shell of the building, by the addition of a handsome and suitable roof, with a richly panelled semi-circular ceiling. That Mr. Thomas Eyre should have been so influenced by kindly feelings towards his Alma Mater, as to be pleased to assist in crowning the lingering work of construction, does not surprise me. That he should have wished to aid in adding one more Catholic Church to the many which have sprung up in England since the Reformation, is only what we might expect from one, who, during the course of his studies at Prior Park, always intended to devote himself, as his brothers Charles, Vincent, John, and William had done, to the service of God in the ecclesiastical state.

The new Church was solemnly opened for divine service on July 6th, 1882. At the opening ceremony, the High Mass was sung by His Lordship the Bishop of Clifton, whose Silver Jubilee was celebrated on the same occasion. The sermon was preached by the Rev. Father Grant, S.J. After the service, luncheon was served to about 250 guests in the hall of the Mansion, and a presentation of an address, with a sum of £930, was made to the Bishop, as a mark of affection from the Catholics of the Diocese on the completion of his twenty-fifth year as Bishop of

Clifton. Lord Arundell of Wardour was one of the spokesmen.

Though the Church is not yet completed, progress is continually being made. The building is entirely composed of Bath stone. On the north and south side, the basement of the Church is formed of an arcade of eleven arches, above which arises one order of the Corinthian style of architecture, between which are the windows lighting the aisles. Above these is a series of panels, which are to be filled with scenes from the lives of SS. Peter and Paul. The porches are at the western ends of the north and south arcades, and upon these will eventually rise two towers, which have at present been carried as high as the belfry floor. The south porch is the public entrance, the north one giving access to St. Paul's College and to the park, and will be used on occasions of processions. The massive doors are of oak, very handsomely carved and panelled. The east end of the building terminates in a semi-circular apse surmounted by a fine dome. The nave is separated from the aisles by a range of very beautiful Corinthian columns raised on pedestals, seven on each side; above these rises the grand cornice, with but a single break on either side, and the nave is covered in with a richly-panelled semi-circular ceiling, the windows lighting the nave being groined into it. Between the pilasters on the walls of the aisles, corresponding with the columns, are arches, blank on the south side, but opening to chapels on the north. The apse is semi-circular, having three-quarter columns round it, and lighted by a lantern in the dome. Overlooking the chancel are two tribunes over the side entrances. The north aisle terminates at the east end in the chapel of the Blessed Sacrament. The south aisle leads to the sacristy, octagonal in form and lighted by a lantern. The organ loft, which has yet to be built, will be at the west end of the nave. The total length of the Church is 120ft., that of the chancel being 43ft.; the breadth of the nave is 27ft. 6in. in the clear of the columns, and the height 45ft. The altar is composed of very rich Italian marbles, the sepulchre for the relics being seen through a beautiful pierced cross of statuary marble. It was made in Rome for the Church, and rests upon three steps, also of marble; at the back is an inscription stating that it was the gift of the Countess English, who also contributed largely towards defraying the cost of the organ. Since the opening of the Church, several beautiful chapels have likewise been opened in the north aisle. The latest is that of St. Edward, richly adorned as a memorial chapel to Monsignor Edward Williams by the Wilmott family.

The next in order is the chapel dedicated to St. John the Evangelist as a memorial to the Very Rev. Dr. John Bonomi; but the altar itself was given by some pupils of Professor James Cavanagh as a memorial of him. On the front of the altar is inscribed, "Ora pro anima Jacobi Cavanagh hujus Collegii Magistri." The next is dedicated to St. Joseph, and is a memorial of Mr. J. J. Scoles, the original architect of the Church, given by his son, the Rev. A. J. Scoles, who is carrying on his father's work. The chapel at the east end of the aisle is a memorial of Archbishop Errington, erected by the Members of the Prior Park Association.

Several of the columns, pedestals, pilasters, balustrades, caps, and much of the carving will be completed at some future date. The Church will accommodate over three hundred persons. Viewed as a whole, the interior of this classic edifice cannot fail to elicit the admiration of all lovers of true art. When completed, the Church will undoubtedly be one of the finest specimens of Italian architecture to be seen in this country.

CHAPTER III.

The Alterations in the Mansion House After the Fire.

I WILL now endeavour to convey to my readers some idea of the plan on which the Mansion was originally built. To effect this I would fain possess a fairy's wand, that so I might, by waving it, be enabled to demolish and build up again at pleasure. Standing in the Portico, I would exert my magic power, and bid the solid masonry of the two magnificent flights of steps vanish into empty space, to be replaced by an old and dingy looking ladder, originally the only available means of communication between the Portico and the terraces below. In the Entrance Hall, another wave of the magic wand would close the opening above with a white ceiling and a boarded floor. Away would go the charming distant vista of the beautiful panelled and ornamented roof; away would go, tenderly borne by fairy hands to some choice corner of fairyland, Archbishop Errington's carefully collected fossils, cases and all.* On the north side, the space on the first floor extended from the Chapel to the end of the Hall would present one lofty and magnifi-

* Since the above sentence was penned, the dear Archbishop's fossils have been transported, not into fairyland, but into what was, in days of old, St. Paul's refectory, and which has been aptly transformed into a museum.

cent library, with elegant bookcases and shelves, and a rich mantelpiece and grate at each end, surmounted by the portraits of Bishop Baines and Pope Leo XII.; the remaining portion of the first floor would be occupied by a passage and an elegant bed-room and dressing-room having a south aspect. Above these would start into existence a long gallery of choice rooms in which any student or contemplative religious might delight to dwell.

Under the changes here signified many beautiful objects would no longer gratify the eye, but the loss would to my mind be insignificant as compared with the advantages that the community would have enjoyed, in the possession of so many commodious rooms as would now exist, had no fire brought about the changes which have been above fancifully reversed. By saying thus much, I seem to be placing myself in a position antagonistic to the better judgment of him who thought proper to deviate from the original plans in the restoration of the building; but it is not so. The Mansion was not reconstructed to serve as a seminary; both the lay and ecclesiastical students were supposed to be sufficiently provided with rooms at St. Paul's College. The Mansion was designed for an episcopal residence. A man in a high and responsible position has to accommodate himself to all classes of society; and Dr. Baines was, by nature and education, well adapted to deal with everybody, and eminently so with those of high rank. To meet the upper classes and to entertain them according to their "status" in society, entered into his large views; hence, whilst contented with comparatively humble rooms himself, his reception rooms were very handsomely furnished, and his mode of receiving and entertaining dignitaries of the Church, the aristocracy, and other distinguished guests, was of that refined character which is never more attractive than when found in combination with the qualities of the dignified ecclesiastic.

The Mansion, besides being intended to meet the requirements of hospitality, was first and foremost an episcopal residence—and this meant more than is at first sight obvious. Bishop Baines was, in every sense of the word, the guiding spirit of his residence. Under his direction, the services of the Church were always carried out with suitable dignity and rubrical exactness. Hence the changes made in the re-construction of the Mansion had for their object the greater solemnity of the services of the Church—even the seemingly superfluous flights of steps leading to the portico were constructed with a view to this same end.

Religious solemnities, imposing in themselves, were doubly so in those days, on account of their novelty. For it must be remembered that Dr. Baines' high aspirations in ceremonial and ecclesiastical matters came at a time when Catholicity in England was in a depressed state, and when, owing to penal prohibitions, chapels had become *quasi* hiding-places, and the external beauty of Catholic worship was unseen and unknown amongst us. Hence crowds of spectators, Catholic and Protestant, were eager to witness what might well be called the ceremonial revival of Catholicism, and it was only when the room above the entrance hall was well filled with individuals, contemplating and admiring a well-conducted procession, on Palm Sunday or Corpus Christi, that the real object which Dr. Baines had in view in introducing an opening in the ceiling of the hall could be rightly understood. It was especially on the feast of Corpus Christi, and during its octave, when both flights of steps were made the scene of a solemn procession of the Blessed Sacrament, that Bishop Baines' leading idea in laying down those steps could also be seized. When Bishop Baines himself, attired in pontifical robes, surrounded by his attendant ministers and bearing the Blessed Sacrament in his hands, ascended to the magnificent portico between long files of surpliced adorers, and gave the solemn benediction for the first time to crowds of the laity massed together on the lower flight, he must have felt himself privileged by the Almighty in being the means by which the beautiful worship of Catholicism was again to be manifested to a nation that had for so long a time been deprived of its old historic faith.

The Mansion was, in some respects, a seminary in which the young ecclesiastic was trained, under the watchful eye of his Bishop, to take his part in the ceremonies of the Church. It was from Bishop Baines that Monsignor Bonomi, for instance, received the training which made him so useful in the Sanctuary; nor was he by any means the only one who acquired a taste for the beautiful and sublime in religion from the same source.

Dr. Baines received his inspirations from the very centre of good taste, in everything connected with collegiate and ecclesiastical architecture. But could he, like Rip Van Winkle, appear among us, after so many years of absence, and see the altered state of things, he would be compelled to allow that his tasteful arrangements and embellishments are beyond the requirements of the day.

Let us now take up our position in front of the steps which lead from the terraces to the Portico, and let us not imagine that these magnificent flights of steps started into existence without much labour and expense. It would be difficult to estimate the cost of them ; but some idea may be gained by considering the large area over which they stretch. In the first place the terraces had to be extended and enlarged, and a grand sweep, such as now exists, had to be given to the slopes, which were to correspond with the lower flight. For this, large quantities of earth were needed, and, fortunately, sufficient was at hand in the excavations which were being made on the south side of the buildings. The land behind the arcades and the refectory of St. Peter's came sloping down towards the buildings themselves, and terminated in a low wall, about three feet high, leaving a passage of about four feet between the low wall and the arcades and refectory. The same was the case, more or less, along the whole line, especially in front of St. Peter's. Hence there was an enormous quantity of earth to be disposed of, and it was a happy coincidence that it could be disposed of to such advantage.

As we look at the steps, four large stone vases catch the eye; hereby hangs a tale. The Rev. Edward Metcalfe, one of the founders of Prior Park College, was the uncle of the genius whose praises are now to be sung. It should be done in blank verse, for he was a youth who thought that he was animated with the spirit of Shakspeare. He wrote tragedies; but I have never heard that any of the tragedies fell into the hands of the printer's devil. He was a painter too. But what has this to do with the four large vases which adorn the steps? Very much; they are the emanations in the concrete of the thoughtful mind and skilful hands of one of the old Prior Park students, who, in his day, was a great favourite, and went by the pet name of "Jimmy" Metcalfe. His real Christian name was Luke. The four vases in question were his *second* attempt at carving and working in stone; an accident led to his making a *first* essay. Mr. Spence, the head mason, was directed to make a vase, which was to be placed in the niche at the end of the arcade near St. Peter's. Mr. Spence was "making bones" about the job, objecting that he was not a sculptor; upon hearing which "Jimmy" Metcalfe, trusting to his genius, joined in and said that, though he had never handled mallet or chisel, *he* would undertake the job. "And if you make anything of it," said Mr. Spence, "I will eat my hat"—a gritty and dusty morsel.

"Let me have a block of stone and tools, and I will try my hand," said "Jimmy." The result was "Jimmy" *did* produce a very respectable foliated vase, which stood in the said niche for many years. Mr. Spence and his family had left Ampleforth with the rest, to follow the fortunes of Dr. Baines; and after superintending the works at Prior Park and taking an active part in them for many years, until all, save the Church, was completed, he died a peaceful death in the adjoining village of Combe Down. He was an honest man, and remarkable for standing by his contracts and completing them, but that he went out of the world without completing his contract with "Jimmy," relative to "eating his hat," is more than probable. I frequently saw "Jimmy" at work carving the four vases. "Jimmy" afterwards went to France, was ordained priest, and was set over a parish. He became a celebrated preacher, the name of "Jimmy" giving place to the more dignified title of Père Metcalfe. The late Lord Clifford was partial to Père Metcalfe. His Lordship visited him on more than one occasion, and brought to England information respecting his whereabouts, etc.

It would be well if there were no more to say about the Mansion, but the subject cannot be dismissed without some sort of description of the fire, which broke out at the end of the month of May, 1836. During the whole of that month no rain had fallen, and the heat had been exceptionally great. This kind of weather naturally rendered the timber in the roof of the Mansion very dry.

It was known that in the building of the Mansion beams of inferior wood had been introduced, merely to counteract the effects of "settlements" in the masonry. Time would make such beams decay, and, if in close proximity to a chimney, a spark falling on them would cause them to smoulder, and eventually to burst into flames.

Dr. Baines, in my hearing, suggested that the fire in the roof of the Mansion may have been due to this cause. But whatever was the origin of the fire, a little boy, Master George Manley, at three o'clock in the afternoon, as the students were leaving the playground for afternoon study, detected smoke issuing from the roof of the Mansion. He endeavoured to call the attention of the Prefect to the fact, who either failed to see the smoke or took no notice of the observations of the child; and so the fire gained ground unobserved, until the boys left the study rooms at a quarter to five o'clock. The smoke was then issuing from the roof unmistakably, and was seen by every eye. The alarm was given, and every available workman on the premises ascended to the top of the roof, and lines were formed by the students and others to pass, from hand to hand, buckets of water, drawn from the nearest pond. The water was thrown upon the hot slates and ran down the spouts, without, of course, producing any visible effect. In the meantime Dr. Baines and his nephew, with more thoughtfulness, rushed to the top gallery, with a view to inspecting the interior of the roof. This was done by entering the first room on the left, and passing through a trap-door in the ceiling. The door of the room was locked, but Mr. James Baines, giving a spring, burst the door open with his foot. Mr. Samuel Spence was directed to climb up and report what he saw.

"It is like a baker's oven," he exclaimed. Had the fire engines been on the spot, and the hose been directed through the trap-door into the burning roof, the Mansion would have been saved ; or had the buckets of water been carried up the stairs, instead of up a ladder on the roof, some good result might have been obtained. But in the meantime Mr. Spence had become alive to the folly of wasting the water on the exterior of the roof, and very unwisely directed the men to open the slates with their pickaxes. This order was fatal ; a draught was now produced, and out burst the flames with redoubled fury. A retreat from the top of the building became necessary, and practically all was over, as far as the preservation of the Mansion was concerned,—and the flames now served as a signal of distress. It was a strong appeal to the inhabitants of Bath for aid, and sympathising friends readily responded to it. The firemen, on their engines, were soon seen galloping through the streets and ascending the hill with all necessary appliances. Hurrying pedestrians made the Prior Park Road more animated than it had ever been before, or perhaps ever will be again ; and what *could* be done doubtless *was* done to arrest the progress of the flames. But to save the *contents* of the house was a more feasible undertaking, and to this every effort was directed. The boys distinguished themselves in saving the books in the library. Mr. George Field took down the organ and saw it carefully packed away. Mr. Spence and his men took down valuable mantel-pieces and placed them in security. Conspicuous on the scene was Don Antonio Rey, the Professor of Theology. He came too *late* to rescue the fruits of many years of hard study, for the fire had caught the ceiling of his room. In his eagerness to save his books and manuscripts, he would probably have perished in the flames, had not Mr. Robert Chapman, afterwards priest of Birkenhead, taken upon himself to save the dear old man's life, and insisted upon his leaving the room immediately.

"Oh! my treatise 'De Ecclesia!'" he cried out; "let me get it!"

"Come along!" was the answer.

Mr. Chapman was too strong to be resisted, and poor Don Antonio, with many treatises in his hand, but not his pet treatise "De Ecclesia," was hustled downstairs to a place of greater safety.

I often heard him lament this irreparable loss.

From this fire Father Hutton had a narrow escape. Many of his books perished; he managed, however, to save from destruction a beautiful Elzevir pocket edition of Cicero, in ten volumes, which is still preserved in the library of Ratcliffe College, with the exception of the third volume, which fell a prey to the flames.

In the year of the foundation of the London University, a new impulse was given to the studies at Prior Park. Students matriculated; and Father Metcalfe, at the request of Dr. Baines, went to

London and purchased educational works to the value of no less than *five hundred pounds*. Some of these probably perished in the flames.

Mr. Chapman was active in looking after the safety of the boys, who continued their work, under his direction, until their exertions became absolutely superfluous. Happily no one sustained any injury, and everything in the way of furniture was rescued. In the meantime the fire raged furiously, and the Mansion was completely destroyed, the basement alone, with its strong stone arches, arresting the course of the conflagration, and resisting the fall of the heavy beams.

Dr. Baines was sitting down to dinner when the alarm of fire was given, and we may imagine the anxiety of his mind during that eventful evening, and his distress when, balanced between hope and fear, he was doomed at last to see himself burnt out of house and home, and compelled to find a resting-place for the night amongst his friends in Bath.

It may be interesting if I here transcribe an account of the fire sent me by an old friend and pupil, who was an eye-witness of the catastrophe :—

"Yes, I am one of the few survivors of those who saw the fire of 1836. The exact date was May 29, which occurred that year on a Saturday. I was in Mr. Chapman's class, with George Coxon, Thos. Clarkson, John Bateman, Costa Ferreira, and two or three others. We were together in the well-known large class-room which stood, and I believe still stands, between the play-room and the old study-place ; and we had just begun our lessons, at about 5 p.m., when Michael Coxon appeared at the glass-door and beckoned mysteriously to our master, who went out, but quickly returned, and bade us 'keep quiet—the house was on fire,' a rather paradoxical and wholly impracticable order to anybody, let alone to little boys. Accordingly we were soon outside, to find ourselves in the midst of confused rushes from the neighbouring class-rooms; but at the bottom of the flight of steps which led down from the terrace-walk, in the rear of St. Peter's, we were stopped by Mr. Furlong (then Prefect), who, in a commanding and long-remembered voice, ordered us 'to go and help at the Mansion,' or something to that effect. Of course we obeyed with alacrity; and indeed by this time everybody had become frantically eager to join in the *melée* and do some service. As we made for the front, several large pieces of furniture and volleys of books came flying out of the windows, which forced us to steer clear of the wall. Dr. Rooker immediately called us up to the library, where we assisted him to carry off as many of the books as could be saved. I think we worked about half an hour, when the fire drove us all back, for even the stairs were no longer safe, and we beat a reluctant retreat to St. Peter's, where a number of the senior boys kept guard against the crowds which had already gathered from Bath and from all directions round about. It must have been shortly afterwards—but in what part of the premises I forget—that I was seized upon by Mr. Langton, a gentleman who lived with his family at No. 1, South Parade,

Bath, and who, as an old friend of my parents, claimed to carry me off to his hospitable home for the night. The mob had by this time reached enormous dimensions. I have heard it computed at ten or eleven thousand; but it was well mastered by the new Police, who had only quite recently come into existence under Peel's Act, and who made, I believe, their very first appearance as a public body at the memorable fire of Prior Park. They showed in large force, and won golden opinions for their admirable maintenance of order, and for the general protection and help afforded by their presence. The mob ranged themselves on the hill behind the Mansion as though in the tiers of an amphitheatre; whence, with eager and countless faces, they scanned for hours the fearful conflagration which was raging below. As Mr. Langton hurried me through this throng, I recollect turning to look back upon the scene; and the figure or semblance of the Bishop recurs to my memory, as he stood there in the front row at the bottom, surrounded by some priests and sympathising friends. I was too young to observe either his countenance or his manner; but he was dressed as for the dinner-table—not in a cassock, but in a frock-coat, and he wore the college cap, with a long purple tassel, which was his habitual covering out of doors when at home. The next day was Sunday, and on that day I was taken back to the College by my grandfather, who also resided in Bath. We entered by the great glass-door, which led, as it still leads, into the central hall. The grand old walls were standing firm as the rock which had borne them, and seemed in nothing injured, save that the fire had blackened all. The glass-door itself, strange to say, escaped well-nigh intact, I believe ; and this was supposed to have happened from the continuous and cooling stream poured on it from so many fire-engines. The hall, however, was one mass of *débris*, the result of fallen beams, combined with the crumbled inside masonry. The rubbish mounted up in some parts to at least twenty feet, and I recollect that in several places it was still smoking. But the fire had been thoroughly got under ; and the Mansion, Phœnix-like, arose speedily from its ashes, and grander and more beautiful than ever it had been."

The Priory was fitted up as soon as possible for Bishop Baines' residence, and there he remained during the rebuilding of the Mansion. Indeed, Miss Crewe, the sister of the present Lord Crewe and aunt to Lord Houghton, the Viceroy of Ireland, was at the Priory at this time, and had already greatly improved it by making additions and putting all in thorough repair, with plate glass windows, etc.

It may not be useless to mention finally that a print of this fire was published some few weeks after the event, by a Bath printing firm. The print gives a fairly accurate idea of the scene in and around the Mansion. The raging flames, the bustling crowd of masters, boys, and sight-seers, the exertions of the firemen, are all limned therein with tolerable accuracy ; and it is still possible, for those who are so minded, to procure an interesting, though melancholy, memorial of a calamity that dealt a terrible blow at the developing prosperity of the College. Such a print may serve to remind all students, past or present, of Prior Park of a prominent landmark in its chequered history.

CHAPTER IV.

The Rebuilding of the Mansion and the Benefactors of the College.

BISHOP BAINES had now to turn his thoughts to the reconstruction of the interior of the destroyed building. It was encouraging to His Lordship to know that the walls had not sustained any material injury. Furthermore he received from the insurance Company two or three thousand pounds. This sum, though far from covering his losses, was most useful. It happened also, providentially, that there was an elegantly built house to be taken down and sold near Shepton Mallet, which went by the name of Houndstreet House. The house built, report says, by Mr. Beckford, was the property of the heir of General Popham. That it was elegant and had been expensively got up may be seen from what was conveyed to Prior Park, viz., the ornamental plaster work in the ceiling of the Central Hall and in the ceilings of several of the rooms in the Mansion, the mahogany doors, pilasters, staircase and banisters, marble chimney pieces, oak boards, etc. But the transport of waggon-loads of building material, besides the ornamental work, must have added considerably to the expense, particularly as there was no railway from Shepton Mallet. From Houndstreet House came laso four pagan statues, which Dr.

Baines endeavoured (through the instrumentality of the Thewenetti brothers and his own devices) to convert into popes and saints. There were three brothers—the eldest, Laurence, was an eminent miniature painter; Michael, the second, was the drawing master at Prior Park from its commencement until its closure; the third, Edward, was a Professor of modern languages and an artist of some merit. None of the Thewenetti brothers were married, and Edward (benefited probably by his brothers' industry as well as by his own thrift) had accumulated sixty thousand pounds.

These statues for some time ornamented the first flight of steps immediately connected with the portico; but, as the covering of cement and canvas, of which the drapery was formed, did not stand the test of weather, the pagan converts gradually fell back into heathenism. The ornamental statuary in the tympanum of St. Peter's, on the north side, also came from Houndstreet House.

Miss Crewe was instructed and received into the Church by Bishop Baines; and the whole course of her life, as connected with Prior Park, gave evidence of a spirit of gratitude and generosity, which prompted her to divest herself of her worldly possessions and employ them in assisting him who had brought her into the Catholic fold. It will probably never be known in this world how much Prior Park is indebted to this good lady; but it is certain that she was a very great benefactress to the College. Amongst gifts which she passed over to it was a large, rare, and valuable collection of paintings, with which the Mansion was decorated. They had been the property of her father. The only painting that remains, from which we may gather some idea of the quality of the collection, is the Crucifixion by Van Dyck in the chapel of the Mansion. This, as already stated, was rescued by Hugh Bateman, Esq., and presented to the College at the restoration. The rest were scattered at the time of the sale of the property. Bishop Clifford, however, shortly before his death, informed me that he was in possession of some of these paintings.

On the death of Dr. Baines, this excellent lady and great benefactress of the College lived in retirement at the Mission House of Tiverton. After her many years of absence from Prior Park, I was one morning much gratified to see her in the chapel of the Mansion, engaged, as of old, in fervent prayer. She had taken possession of the Priory again, and, from her suffering state, one might have been led to conclude that she had returned to Prior Park to end her days in the midst of those scenes, which had lent a charm and given an interest to her Catholic life. She died on the 4th of February, 1879.

It would be an injustice to the memory of the Very Rev. Monsignor Thomas Brindle, not to class him among the early benefactors of Prior Park College. He was the constant friend of Bishop Baines, and the only official who remained at the College from its commencement to its dissolution. Whatever he possessed was freely thrown into the coffers of Bishop Baines, for the College—and I learn from Provost Brindle that his uncle's possessions were very considerable, amounting to between nine and ten thousand pounds. Like Bishop Baines, he gave up all he had for the benefit of Prior Park, leaving nothing behind him ; and if kind friends had not come forward to minister to his wants in the decline of life, his sun would have set in the midst of the dark clouds of sorrow and privation.

There was an old gentleman of the name of Mennel, who came to Prior Park with the Superiors of Ampleforth College. He belonged to the industrious and thrifty class of Catholics, who save a competency for old age and bequeath it to the Church. He possessed a few thousand pounds. Provost Brindle, of Barnstaple, said that the first flight of steps from the portico was paid for by him, and that he gave all that he possessed to the College.

The spirit of the founders of Prior Park, and of their immediate friends, was one of self-sacrifice and disinterestedness. The hard working professors of the Institute of Charity asked for no remuneration beyond food and raiment, and the other ecclesiastical teachers, for the most part, served on the same terms. And if early success, and the approval and support of the Catholic public, may be taken as a guarantee that every man did his duty, and that the great venture of Dr. Baines' episcopacy was well timed, such guarantee was not wanting. But the noble institution was launched on the uncertain ocean of time, and the accidents which have brought other great works to nought affected it; for the early death of its founder, the rocks and shoals of adversity, broke it up and scattered its fragments to be picked up by any passer-by. But He who said to His disciples, "Gather up the fragments that remain, lest they be lost," has, through the instrumentality of a successor of the same Apostles and his fellow-labourers, "gathered in those fragments," and that which was disjointed and fast running to waste, in the noble institution is again assuming a compact and stable form.

Many a wounded spirit has exclaimed in the hour of distress, "Master, we have laboured all the night and have taken nothing," and the practical answer, with the well-known successful result, has been, "Launch out into the deep and let down your nets again for a draught." And let those whose hearts must beat feverishly at times, under the weight of responsibility attached to the work of restoration, take courage from the concluding words of Our Lord to Simon, "Fear not; from henceforth thou shalt catch men."

CHAPTER V.

ST. PETER'S COLLEGE—

THE TRAINING OF THE SCHOLARS IN ELOCUTION.

LET us now turn to St. Peter's College. Passing through the inside corridor, we arrive at the semi-circular class-room on the left and the large class-room on the right. These two rooms, with the passage between them, formed, "in the beginning," one large room, which was used for a lecture-room, concert-room, and theatre—the stage occupying the large class-room on the right. The opening above was for ventilation, and the dormitory around the opening served for the orchestra. Mr. Manners conducted the music there, and thus the singers and instrumentalists were out of the way, leaving the available space below for the distinguished audience. Our first performance was "Julius Cæsar," Moses Furlong being the Brutus of the day, and the animating spirit of the whole. Dr. Baines was our patron in every sense of the word. Moses Furlong solicited the aid of Mr. Bellamy, the manager of the Bath Theatre, who gave him some very good hints and provided us with dresses. Before saying more, I will observe that the theatre was a modification of a brew-house—one of the offices belonging to the Mansion. Like so many ceilings in the buildings at Prior Park, the roof was arched with stone and surmounted with a dome, which dome, with no small trouble to the builder, was raised high in the air, on the top of St. Peter's, previous to the changes made in the building itself.

Before the completion of the theatre, the plays were acted in the library, in the Mansion. On one occasion the elder students acted scenes from "Cato," and the junior students scenes from "Henry IV." Hotspur was well played by an Irish boy of the name of O'Neil, who was said to be "equal to the young Roscius." An excellent string band, conducted by the eminent John Loder, of Bath, enlivened the performance. Dr. Baines took a lively interest in everything connected with the stage, and the inhabitants of Bath were much pleased with these representations. Indeed, the refined taste for elocution possessed by the founder of the College, and his high appreciation of the value of good speaking, gave to our renderings of the plays of Shakespeare an educational importance, upon which he always strongly insisted. It was a saying of Dr. Baines that "the world is ruled by orators;" and we had the advantage of continually listening to those sermons, which, as I have already mentioned, were so highly appreciated by His Eminence Cardinal Wiseman with regard to their "easy flow of words, their imagery, their elegance, and their elocution in general." Without being aware of it, perhaps, the young men caught up His Lordship's enthusiasm for the oratorical art, and endeavoured to imitate his manner of speaking. Moses Furlong (afterwards Father Furlong, of the Institute of

Charity) derived the greatest benefit from constantly observing and studying His Lordship's mode of delivery, and he became himself a popular missionary preacher, and was considered to be an apt pupil, in this respect, of Dr. Baines. He studied the art of elocution also under the well-known Liverpool actor, Mr. Vandenhoff, and became a most energetic and indefatigable teacher of elocution at the College. When Father Furlong left, the task of teaching elocution devolved upon me, and I have ever since taken a prominent part in preparing the Prior Park boys for their plays and exhibitions. Not relying wholly on myself, I sought the aid of the best teachers of elocution I could find. Hence Mr. Barton, a first-class Professor, was introduced by me to the authorities at Prior Park, and it will be remembered that Mr. Barton was a very efficient teacher and an amiable and gentlemanly man.

My efforts to keep up the traditional spirit of elocution at Prior Park are known and appreciated by many of the "past students" of the College, and it has been a source of great pleasure to hear some of them say that the lessons on elocution which they received during the preparation of the plays of Shakespeare for public exhibition were not only a source of pleasure at the time, but a real benefit to them in after-life. Mr. James Fox and his brother Charles distinguished themselves, the former in the character of Hamlet and the latter in playing the part of the King. Both became eminent speakers, and are still pleading at the Bar. Mr. James Parfitt, owing to his powerful and sonorous voice, and his unusually developed physical frame—he stands six feet four inches—made an impressive ghost in the play of "Hamlet." His final appearance on the College stage was in the character of Macbeth, his stepping-stone to the Bar. He is a distinguished speaker, and in full practice at the present time.

The decline of life still finds me at my work of inculcating the art of elocution, and recent successes proclaim my undying zeal in the good cause. Whatever *good* I may have done in keeping alive the traditions of the College respecting elocution, by putting on the stage at Prior Park such plays of Shakespeare as "Julius Cæsar," "Macbeth," "Hamlet," "The Merchant of Venice," etc., will, I hope, be treasured up and improved upon by those of my pupils who are now in responsible positions at the College. I would have the benefit, derived from my teaching, regarded as a deposit to bear interest in the improvement of the present and future generations, but especially in the propagation of a good style of pulpit oratory, to the advantage of religion and the honour and glory of God. It is really quite impossible to overstate the importance and utility of preaching, especially in the apathetic times in which we live. Our priests may not be able to become Lacordaires or Monsabrés ; but they can do very much in the direction of adapting their subject-matter to the pressing spiritual needs of the day, and perfecting its oral delivery. Hence arises the necessity of a conscientious study of the art of elocution, without adequate knowledge of which the preacher cannot expect to exert a stirring religious influence upon the minds of his hearers. "*Proficiat ars tantis virtutibus impleta.*"

The semi-circular class-room to which I have drawn attention, the chapel, the centre portion of St. Peter's, and the play-room are the original sites of the old offices appertaining to the Mansion. The class-rooms and the rooms on the north side, the ambulacrum and the lavatory and swimming-bath, are all additions to the original structure. The walls of the old offices, as in St. Paul's College, were strong enough to support the super-structure as it now stands. The lavatory of St. Peter's College was divided into three rooms, which were occupied by Bishop Baines when the Superiors and students from Ampleforth first arrived at Prior Park, on the 27th of May, 1830—the small octagon room serving the purpose of His Lordship's domestic chapel.

At a very early period St. Peter's College narrowly escaped being burnt to the ground, and it was the quick eye of a little boy that saved it. The boys under the charge of Mr. Furlong, the Prefect, had assembled in the large upper room facing the north. It being winter, there was a lighted stove, around which we had gathered to listen to one of Mr. Furlong's interesting tales. We had actually risen and were leaving the room, when the little boy exclaimed, "I see fire under the boards!" and, indeed, through a crevice in the boards the fire was conspicuous enough. The warning was not neglected. The fire in the stove was put out, and the stove itself removed from its position. The boards underneath the stove and the joists on which they rested were ignited. Had not the fire been discovered and speedily arrested, it is fearful to think what might have occurred in the dead of the night, the dormitories being below and there being no one in the rooms above to give the alarm. Dr. Baines himself was soon on the spot, and did not leave until he was fully satisfied that all was safe.

Leaving St. Peter's College and turning to the left, we arrive at the spacious terrace constructed by Dr. Baines. At the end of the terrace is a very substantial building and ball-place, erected by the Rev. James Baines, nephew to the Bishop. These buildings, being constructed in the quarry from which the stones were taken, cost only £300, though under ordinary circumstances they would have cost upwards of £1,000. The flat roof was intended originally to serve as a watch-tower, from which the Prefect had a commanding view of the "bounds" and the "tennis-court." The rooms below were intended for reading-rooms in wet weather and for imposition-rooms. At present they are occupied by the "ground-man" and his wife, the latter of whom acts as nurse in any dubious case of illness, the building then serving as a place of isolation. The ball-place was very much used in the early days, when hand-ball was so popular, but for nearly forty years the court has remained alienated from its original purposes, and is at present used for a poultry yard.

CHAPTER VI.

The Athletic Sports of Early Days.

WE will now go back fifty-four years and see how the athletic sports of the College were conducted in the adjoining grounds. On Tuesday, May 22nd, 1849, "our boys" held their Spring Meeting in true sporting style, as may be seen by the printed list, which I have before me, of the names and colours of the competitors in the races. They had their Stewards of the Races, their Paulite Cup, their Union Plate, their Handicap, their Liliputian Stakes, their Tally-ho Sweepstakes (a hurdle race), etc. The Stewards were A. J. Biddulph, Esq., Edward Williams, Esq., and L. B. English, Esq. The Judge was E. B. Pitchford, Esq. The following is a sample of two or three of the "events" as given in the programme :—

THE PRIORY GREAT HANDICAP.

Open to all subscribers of one shilling each. Heats to be run in two lots; the first three of each lot to run again together. The winner of the last heat to receive a prize of one guinea, the second in the same a prize of the value of seven shillings (both the gift of the Priory), the third to save his stake. The winner is disqualified for the Tally-ho Sweepstakes. Twenty entries, seventeen "acceptances." 120 yards.

Mr. William's "*Pretty Good Speed*" (white body, scarlet sleeves and cap).

Mr. Biddulph's "*Corsair.*"

Mr. Guibara's "*Harkaway.*"

"*Pretty Good Speed*" came in second.

LILIPUTIAN STAKES.

Value eight shillings. The second a donation from the Racing Fund.

Mr. Chas. Bunbury's "*Lightning*" (white body, blue and white cap).

Mr. James William's "*Young Lion.*"

Mr. Chas. Graham's "*Little Wonder.*"

"*Lightning*" came in first.
"*Young Lion*" second.

THE TALLY-HO SWEEPSTAKES.

Of one shilling each.

Mr. William's "*Man in the Moon*" (white, scarlet sleeves and cap).

Mr. Russell's "*Eighty-Four*" (white, blue cap).

"*Man in the Moon,*" in later days the Right Rev. Monsignor Williams, D.D., came in first. "*Eighty-Four*" came in second. Only a few names are here given out of many.

Perhaps the youths of the Colleges of SS. Peter and Paul may estimate their skill in running and leaping as, at least, equal to that of the racers of 1849; but are they so well in advance in their studies as to give promise that they will eventually vault to the high positions in society to which some of their predecessors attained—will they become Archbishops, Bishops, Generals, and Heads of Colleges? To sport is one thing and to study is another; but the two pursuits may be so combined as to act as a kind of genuine recreation to each other. It was this harmonious combination of play and study that produced in the minds of the old Prior Park boys those powers which led to such brilliant successes in the Church, in the Army, the law, and important mercantile pursuits.

The students of the present generation have in their keeping the future well-being of their Alma Mater. What might, perchance, have been the altered position of Prior Park if "The Man in the Moon" and "Young Lion" had not been good boys and good students, as well as good runners and good leapers? Who amongst the Prior Park students is to be the future Bishop of the Clifton Diocese? Who the President and who the Vice-President of the College? Who the Professor of Theology? All these positions, and many others, are open to all comers, and may the young gentlemen of this age so run, "not as at an uncertainty," and may they so fight, not "as beating the air," but as successfully coping with those difficulties, moral and intellectual, which stand between them and the high and responsible positions in life to which I have alluded, and to which I trust they may attain.

CHAPTER VII.

Some Recent Benefactors of the College.

IT is now my agreeable duty to speak of the recent benefactors of the College.

The Countess English, as a benefactress to Prior Park, must needs be remembered with gratitude by all who are attached to the College. She was born on the 5th of February, 1814; and, inasmuch as her mother (*née* Frances Huddleston) was of the ancient and illustrious family of the Huddlestons of Millum Castle, in the county of Cumberland, and of Sawston Hall, in Cambridgeshire, she was nobly born. (See "Burke's Royal Families of England," Volume 2nd, Pedigree CXXXIV.)

In the year 1811 Frances Huddleston was married to Mr. John English, who in his day was an eminent solicitor and an alderman of Bath. He was the solicitor of Dr. Baines in the purchase of Prior Park, and in other legal transactions connected with the College. Mr. English's family was likewise a good old Catholic family residing in Lancashire.

Thus descended, Isabella Jane English, afterwards made Countess by His Holiness Pope Pius IX., had imbibed from early childhood strong Catholic tendencies, accompanied with a corresponding aversion to every form of heresy, and her whole life was a practical proof of her ardent desire to advance the best interests of the Church.

Here I would wish to draw the attention of the friends of the College to the fact that Prior Park is indirectly indebted to Miss Elizabeth Dalton, of Thurnham Hall, Lancashire, for the benefactions which the Trustees of the College ultimately received, through the generosity of the Countess English. The mother of the Countess had, during her school days, been the friend and companion of young Miss Dalton. About three years before the death of Mr. Dalton in the year 1837, Mrs. English went with her daughter Isabella Jane on a visit to Thurnham Hall; and during her short stay there, her daughter found such favour with Miss Dalton, that it was eventually arranged that Miss Isabella Jane should take up her abode there.

When Miss Dalton, on the demise of her father, came into possession of Thurnham Hall, she adopted her friend Isabella English, and constituted her heiress of her own personal property, the value being about £100,000. This the Countess looked upon as a deposit, of which she would have to render an account; and giving up many light and interesting occupations, musical and artistic, she gave her attention to such studies as would enable her to become a good accountant, and to manage her own property.

It is largely to her business habits, her order, and tact (which gained her the respect of bankers, brokers, and solicitors) that Prior Park owes the large sum of ready money which the Countess gave to the Trustees of the College, to enable them to arrest the downward tendency of the College, consequent upon the continuous dilapidations of half a century and more.

Even before her death the Countess continually assisted His Lordship the Bishop and Monsignor Williams in their difficulties. The handsomely-carved oak sideboard in the refectory and the oak panelling around was her gift. She was, also, the donor of the marble High Altar in the Church; and she so far assisted in the purchase of the organ that, without her intervention, it would probably not be where it is. The deed of gift of £2,000 for a Theological Chair was made previously to her death, which occurred on the 2nd of September, 1888, at the age of 74.

Since her death the Trustees have found themselves in a position to place the College, in point of comfort, on a footing with other establishments of the kind. The covered tepid swimming bath and the elegant lavatory at St. Peter's could scarcely be improved upon. They are, in every respect, fitted up with a view to utilising all modern improvements. The pier-glasses, which form a portion of the decorations of the luxurious lavatory, belonged formerly to Her Ladyship's drawing-room at Regent's Park, London.

The Right Rev. Monsignor Parfitt was another of the recent benefactors to Prior Park, and it is to him that the College owes the exquisite mahogany furniture and bookcases, filled with valuable books, which make several rooms, of the previously desolate Mansion, so pleasant to look upon. But what has been hitherto given, though very munificent, is probably a mere prelude to what is in store for Prior Park and the Clifton Diocese, through his instrumentality.

A short sketch of the history of this great benefactor, and of the ways of Divine Providence in his regard, cannot but prove interesting.

Mr. Charles Parfitt, of the ancient family of Parfitt, of Bruton, Somerset (see "Burke's Authorised Arms," p. 133), came to Prior Park in the early days of the College, and was one of those who assisted Dr. Baines in its establishment. He was a convert, and was received into the Church by Dr. Combes, of Shepton Mallet. He afterwards became the President of St. Peter's College, which was full to overflowing. Soon after his ordination to the priesthood, he was appointed chaplain to Mr. Conolly, of Midford Castle, near Bath, and became an intimate friend of the family.

As Mr. Conolly died without issue, the disposal of the Midford Estate became subject to Mrs. Conolly, his mother, who was a widow. The power vested in her she used in favour of her friend, the Right Rev. Monsignor Parfitt, D.D. After her death the will was disputed, but Monsignor Parfitt gained his cause. This litigation, however, crippled the estate to a very great extent.

It was well known that Mr. Conolly, having no family, freely raised money on the estate; and Monsignor Parfitt by no means inherited the Midford Estate in its entirety. Indeed he declared that he received only £500 per annum from it. Mr. Conolly's wife, the Marchesa di St. Agata, continued and still continues to inhabit Midford Castle; Monsignor Parfitt was her chaplain till his death on the 27th of June, 1886, when he bequeathed the property to the Bishop. The spiritual wants of Midford are now supplied from Prior Park.

Another of the recent benefactors of the College is Sir George Errington, Bart., of Lackham, Chippenham. It was he who supplied the funds for the completion of the cloister where Archbishop Errington and Monsignor Edward Williams are buried. The memorial chapel for the Archbishop was paid for by the Members of the Prior Park Association.

Archbishop Errington's first connection with Prior Park seems to have been when he was translated from the Bishopric of Plymouth to the Archiepiscopal See of Trebizond in 1855. It was he that wound up the affairs of the College at the beginning of 1856, during the interval between the death of Bishop Burgess, in 1854, and the appointment of Bishop Clifford, in 1857. He seems to have been especially selected by the Pope for this difficult task on account of his business qualifications and great ability. About the year 1874, Archbishop Errington came, in his 70th year, to live a life of retirement at the College. Whilst paying liberally for his board and residence, he gave his invaluable services as Professor of Theology. He died at the College on the 19th of January, 1886, leaving to Prior Park his large collection of valuable books, as well as his fine collection of geological specimens. The Archbishop was certainly a benefactor to the College in more senses than one, but whether he bequeathed any money to it I have not been informed. The architectural improvements, however, made at Prior Park by Sir George Errington, in honour of his distinguished uncle, are certainly indirectly due to the good Archbishop.

Whilst on the subject of recent benefactors and benefactions, mention must be made of the spacious gymnasium, at St. Paul's College, fitted up with all the modern appliances. This building seems to crown the works which have been recently accomplished at Prior Park, to secure health and recreation to its inmates. The expenses of the gymnasium were defrayed by a collection among the friends of the late President, Monsignor Edward Williams, whose latest expressed desire was that a gymnasium should be erected in the College. Connected with this, as a memorial, is the gift of the Misses Wilmott, of the beautiful marble altar in St. Edward's Chapel. The marbles are rich and exquisitely blended, and the altar, taken as a whole, is said to be equal to anything of its kind, even in Italy. The chapel is a memorial chapel, fitted up by the said ladies as a mark of esteem and regard for their revered friend, the late Right Reverend Monsignor Edward Canon Williams, B.A., D.D., etc., President of Prior Park for twenty-four years.

One of the recent benefactors of the College was the Abbate Ferrera, a good and learned Italian priest, who died at the Convent of Franciscan Nuns, at Clevedon. He was much attached to our Bishop, and gave him all he possessed. It is partly to him that the College housekeeper owes the replenishment of her safes, cupboards, etc.;

but it is chiefly to Monsignor Parfitt and the Countess English that Mrs. Campbell owes her abundant supply of valuable silver plate, antique china and crockery, tumblers, wine-glasses, decanters, etc., which she has now always ready at hand to grace the festive board.

Bishop Baines, speaking to a Rosminian Father in days of old, said, "Out of the fifty thousand pounds which I have spent on Prior Park, five thousand came from my Diocese." We may say that the fifty thousand pounds are still represented (in a somewhat dilapidated form) in the noble structure of Prior Park; and when it comes, in course of time, to be repaired and put in thorough working order, those who have repined over the comparatively small loss inflicted by Bishop Baines on his Diocese will surely be generous enough to allow that, in the long run, he has been its most disinterested benefactor. The work of restoration is going on apace, and there is every reason to believe that, in a few years, the fondest hopes of the great founder of the College will have been realised, and even, if possible, surpassed.

The views of Dr. Baines in reference to the advancement of Catholic education in England were of a comprehensive character, and his expenditure was in accordance with his views; but, under the watchful care of Divine Providence, nothing that he expended has been lost to religion. The original cost of the Estate and buildings of Prior Park was £22,000. Bishop Clifford repurchased it, with all the additions and improvements made by Dr. Baines, for £23,000.

CHAPTER VIII.

A Short Memoir of Monsignor Edward Williams.

THIS chapter must be devoted to a sketch of the life and character of the Right Rev. Monsignor Edward Canon Williams, D.D., President of Prior Park College from its revival on April 23rd, 1867, to his own death on March 9th, 1891.

Edward Williams was born at Crinda, near Newport, in Monmouthshire, on the 2nd of March, 1831. As he was a pious boy and gave signs of a vocation to the priesthood, he was sent to Prior Park in his thirteenth year. "He was studious," said Bishop Clifford in his funeral sermon, "and had a great yearning for knowledge; he often used to speak with affection of the Rev. John Brande Morris, who was a distinguished scholar, and one of the masters of Prior Park, who imbued him with a great love for the classics. He had a considerable taste for music, in the cultivation of which he was encouraged and aided by Monsignor James Shepherd. Having completed his course of classical studies, and having now fully resolved to serve God in the priesthood, he studied theology under the Rev. Dr. Rooker, who was President of the College. He had scarcely completed his course when the pecuniary difficulties under which Prior Park had been for some time struggling reached their culminating point, and it was found necessary to close the College, and its inmates were dispersed.

This was in the year 1855. Edward Williams was then ordained priest by Archbishop Errington, who had lately been appointed administrator of the Diocese of Clifton. He had always entertained a warm affection for his Alma Mater, and he was greatly grieved by the breaking up of the College and the loss of Prior Park to the Diocese. He was destined to hold a foremost place in the work of its restoration at a later period. It is related of him that, when he first came to the College as a small boy, the Rev. Mr. Metcalfe, who brought him from Wales, in presenting him to the Rev. Mr. Shattock, at the time head of the school, said, 'Sir, I bring you a new boy; take care of him, for he will one day take your place,' words which, in the event, proved prophetic. After his ordination he went to reside at Frome, as second priest with the Rev. Richard Ward (afterwards Canon Ward), and under him served for some time the double mission of Frome and Chippenham."

When Dr. Clifford was appointed Bishop of Clifton (1857), recognising the rare qualities of the Rev. Edward Williams, he sent him to Rome to pursue a higher course of theological studies. In due time he took his degree of Doctor of Divinity, and, on returning to England, he was soon appointed to the head-mastership of a Catholic Grammar School, which the Bishop had recently opened at Clifton. In 1863 he was elected Canon of the Cathedral Chapter, and later on he was appointed Canon Theologian. In 1866 the Bishop re-purchased Prior Park, and on the

23rd of April, 1867, the Professors and students moved into their new home. Dr. Williams found Prior Park in a dilapidated condition and the Church roofless; but, nothing daunted, he worked steadily on, and now all is changed, and prosperity has dawned upon the College. He was eagerly looking forward to the celebration of the silver jubilee of the re-opening of the College, but he died in the twenty-fourth year after that event, on the 9th of March, 1891, at the age of 60.

The honours conferred upon him show the high opinion in which he was held by his ecclesiastical superiors. Besides the honours already mentioned, he had the honour of being named Private Chamberlain to His Holiness Pope Pius IX., and the present Holy Father granted him the higher dignity of Domestic Prelate.

It may be mentioned that, while studying at Prior Park, he took the degree of Bachelor of Arts of the University of London, with first class classical honours.

The handsome portrait of Monsignor Edward Williams, which now hangs in the entrance hall of the Mansion, was painted by Charles Lovell, Esq., of London, one of the recent Prior Park students, and pupil of Mr. Hobson, of Bath—a Professor of drawing at the College of long standing. It was paid for by subscription at the same time as the gymnasium was erected.

Monsignor Williams has been succeeded by his brother, Monsignor James Williams, B.A., who has always been his *alter ego* in the work of the College of Prior Park.

CHAPTER IX.

DEATH OF BISHOP CLIFFORD, AUGUST 14TH, 1893.

IT is sad to think that the last chapter of my Reminiscences should be written to record the death of our good Bishop. He was everything to us; he resuscitated Prior Park, and took the most lively interest in everything connected with it; hence every member of the College practically feels his loss, down to the smallest child who was favoured with his smiles.

The blow was in some respects sudden. The bitter chalice of death was placed before him in the form of a dangerous operation. There was a chance of life, but he prepared for death by receiving the last Sacraments, in full consciousness of what was before him.

He walked from his sick-room into the small oratory in the Mansion Chapel, and himself directed the ceremony of the last anointing. He made his profession of faith, and said prayers aloud suitable to the occasion. It was a most edifying and impressive scene, and I may say unprecedented. The ceremony finished, he returned to his room to pass through the fearful ordeal. I myself was present on the occasion, and Monsignor Williams administered the Extreme Unction, assisted by the Bishop's constant friend and secretary, Canon Russell.

It is consoling to think that everything was

done that could be done to save the august patient's life; and, when that was beyond the power and skill of man, to soothe his passage through the dreary and painful hours which preceded his death.

The operation, performed by Dr. Fenwick, a specialist from London, was as successful under the circumstances as it could be, whilst the unremitting attention of Mr. King, day and night, was beyond all praise. His Lordship was nursed with affectionate care and solicitude by his sister, the Hon. Mrs. Kavanagh, and by two sisters from the Clifton Wood Convent; and that his religious consolations might be complete, a telegram conveying the Blessing of the Pope arrived during his last moments.

The deceased prelate was the second surviving son of Hugh Charles, seventh Baron Clifford, of Chudleigh, and was born at Irnham, on Christmas Eve, 1823. His mother was the only daughter of the late Thomas Weld, who, after his wife's death, took holy orders and became a Cardinal. After studying for a time at Hodder, Stonyhurst, he then went to Prior Park, Bath, and afterwards to the College "dei Ecclesiastici Nobili," in Rome, where, in 1840, he came under the notice of Gregory XVI., by delivering in his presence, on August 15th, a Latin panegyric on the Blessed Virgin. The Hon. Mr. Clifford was ordained sub-deacon, at Bruges, on the 2nd, and deacon on the 26th of July, 1849; but his promotion to the priesthood was accomplished at Clifton, Bristol, in the Church of the Twelve Apostles, by Bishop

Hendren, Vicar Apostolic of the Western District, on August 25th, 1850. He remained attached to the Church of his ordination until September 16th, 1851, when he returned to Rome, and took his degree as Doctor of Divinity.

He then came back to England, and in April, 1852, joined Dr. Errington, then recently consecrated the first Bishop of Plymouth, as secretary, and later on as head priest at St. Mary's, Stonehouse. He accompanied His Lordship to the first Provincial Council, at Oscott, in July, 1852, and was appointed one of its three secretaries. Upon the erection of the Plymouth Chapter on Nov. 26th, 1853, Dr. Clifford was appointed Canon, and on December 6th was installed Canon Theologian, becoming secretary as well as treasurer to the Chapter, to whom he generously presented the official seal, designed by Mr. Charles Weld, of Chideock. When Bishop Errington was raised to the titular-Archbishopric of Trebizond, and made coadjutor to Cardinal Wiseman, Archbishop of Westminster, by Pius IX.'s Brief of March 30th, 1855, Dr. Clifford was, on May 16th, elected Vicar Capitular of the Plymouth Diocese (that is, an ecclesiastic who takes the place of a Bishop until a new one is appointed), and in this capacity he assisted at the second Provincial Council, held at Oscott two months later. When the brief, dated July 10th, 1855, appointed William (Canon) Vaughan, of Clifton, to the vacant See of Plymouth, Dr. Clifford became his Vicar General; but when His Lordship had been consecrated, and had taken possession of his See on Sept. 25th, Dr.

Clifford proceeded to Rome to finish a course of Canon Law. Early in 1857 he was appointed to the See of Clifton, which had remained vacant since the death of Bishop Burgess on Nov. 27th, 1854, but which had been administered meanwhile by Archbishop Errington as Administrator Apostolic. Dr. Clifford was thus the third Bishop of Clifton. He was consecrated by Pius IX. himself, in the Vatican, on February 15th, 1857, and nominated Assistant at the Throne on March 3rd following. By the year 1880 he had re-established Prior Park as a college, greatly embellished the Pro-Cathedral at Clifton, and made himself a reputation for ecclesiastical and archæological erudition. He was often employed as confidential representative of the English Bishops in important affairs at Rome.

He was a learned theologian, and from his extensive acquaintance with the Canon Law, and the very intricate usages of the Catholic Church, he was constantly referred to by his brother Bishops to transact business with the hierarchy at Rome. He was never more happy than in that city, and spoke the Italian language as fluently as a cultivated native of the peninsula. Much of his time, in fact, was spent in Rome, in affairs which would not be made known through ordinary channels.

The Bishop was in Rome as recently as the commencement of 1893, when he accompanied Cardinal Vaughan, and, as is well known, did a great deal to facilitate the arrangements made for those who visited the city on the occasion of the English pilgrimage conducted by the Duke of Norfolk.

During his episcopate great progress was made in the erection of churches throughout the Diocese, while numerous missions were opened and school-houses built. The whole work of the Diocese was, in fact, greatly developed under the Bishop, who was an excellent organiser.

Of unassuming manners, the Bishop was much beloved by all who knew him for his amiability of disposition, and he possessed a profound and varied acquaintance with several subjects. His great delight, outside the duties appertaining to his office, was in archæology, and he was a frequent attendant at the meetings of the Somersetshire and Gloucestershire Societies.

The Funeral.

August 18th, 1893, with the imposing ceremonial with which the Catholic Church accompanies the funerals of its high ecclesiastical dignitaries, the body was laid to rest at Prior Park, in the tomb in which repose the remains of the late Archbishop Errington—a resting-place which he himself had chosen.

On Tuesday the 15th, the body was removed from the death-chamber to the Chapel in the Mansion, where it lay in state until Wednesday afternoon, robed in full episcopal vestments, the head being covered with a white linen mitre, and the hands, above the breast, clasping a crucifix, rosary, and a small brass figure of the Blessed Virgin. All Monday night, and until the final ceremonial, the coffin was watched by mourners, and during certain hours large numbers of visitors filed through the Chapel to pay their last solemn tribute.

The obsequies commenced on Thursday evening at 7 o'clock, with a solemn dirge, the body having been previously removed from the Mansion House Chapel to the College Church.

Here it was received by the President of the College, the Right Rev. Monsignor Williams, who, with the usual ceremonial, proceeded to the catafalque, where the sad burden was placed immediately in front of the High Altar, and surrounded with tall candles. The lid of the coffin was surmounted in the centre by a brass Roman cross and two shields. One was emblazoned with the deceased's family coat of arms, and the other bore the following inscription :—

A.D. XIX. KAL. SEP. AMVI. MDCCCCXIII.
ÆTATIS SUÆ LXX.
IN CHRISTO DECESSIT
GULIELMUS JOSEPHUS HUGO
EX BARONIBUS CLIFFORD
EPISCOPUS CLITTONIENSIS
R.I.P.

The time appointed for the Requiem Mass the next day was 11 o'clock, and punctually on the stroke of 11 the celebrant, Bishop Graham, ascended the altar steps. The five Bishops present wore black copes and white mitres.

Among the family mourners who took up their places on entering the Church on either side of the catafalque were the present Lord Clifford, of Ugbrooke Park (nephew of the Bishop), the Hon. Mrs. Kavanagh, of Leamington (sister), the Hon. and Rev. Walter Clifford (brother), the Duke of Norfolk, Sir Edward Vavasour, Count and Countess de Torre Diaz (niece of the Bishop), Mr. Edwin de Lisle (cousin), Mr. Henry Clifford (nephew), Lord and Lady Denbigh, Sir Francis and Lady Fleming, Mr. Edward Vavasour (nephew), Sir Walter Blunt and Lord Arundell of Wardour (cousins).

Besides the priests of the Diocese and of Prior Park, the various religious orders of the Diocese were all represented : the Franciscans, from Bristol and Clevedon ; the Fathers of the "Sacred Heart," from Glastonbury ; the Fathers of the Immaculate Conception, from Devizes ; the Benedictines, from Downside, Bath, and Cheltenham ; the Jesuits, from Bristol ; and the Carmelites, from Wincanton. A number of sisters from the Clifton Wood Convent were also in attendance at the funeral.

In the procession to the sanctuary, the priests were followed by the cross-bearer, acolytes, and the canons in their mozettas and rochets, the five prelates and the celebrant in the rear. His Worship the Mayor of Bath (Alderman Murch) attended the ceremonial, accompanied by the Town Clerk (Mr. John Stone). Both were seated just outside the sanctuary on the left-hand side of the altar, in chairs provided by themselves, the Mayor wearing his chain of office.

The musical service was conducted by Canon Barron, of Gloucester, a number of the choir of Gloucester Cathedral assisting. The music was plain chant, unaccompanied, and this, combined with the mournful surroundings, produced a very solemn effect.

Dr. Hedley was the preacher, and, speaking

from the draped rostrum immediately outside the sanctuary, he delivered an impressive discourse of 35 minutes' duration, based on the words, "O Lord, Thou who hast tried me and know me," *Psalm* cxxxviii. 1.

At the conclusion of the panegyric, the five absolutions were chanted in succession by the celebrant and the four other prelates, each Bishop walking round the catafalque, incensing and sprinkling holy water on the coffin. The absolutions are strictly not absolutions, but prayers for the repose of the soul of the person on whose behalf the Requiem is celebrated. After this solemn function, the bearers approached the catafalque, and no portion of the elaborate ceremonial was more effective than the procession of priests, each with a burning taper in his hand, filing slowly down the aisle, with the worshippers on each side sitting in comparative gloom. As the procession left the Church on its way to the tomb in the south cloister, M. Nourry gave an effective rendering of the Dead March in *Saul.* The coffin was then borne to the tomb just outside the Church, the choir and clergy chanting the "In Paradisum"—"May the angels bring thee to Paradise." The grave was afterwards blessed by Bishop Graham, the remains deposited, and the Benedictus sung to very solemn music, the priests and those who had followed the corpse to the Church one by one sprinkling holy water upon the coffin. So ended the ceremony—as sad as it was grand and impressive—and the procession of Bishops and priests returned to the Mansion.

The floral tributes were not numerous, in accordance with request, but there were many beautiful wreaths surrounding the coffin as it lay upon the catafalque. Among those who forwarded mementoes were Mr. Austin J. King and family, Lady Pollen (of Stroud), Mr. Walter Poole (Bridgwater), Mrs. Smyth Pigott (Brockley), Mrs. Ruscombe Poole (Clevedon), and Miss Southeby. Others were received from the Convent of Mercy, Dighton street, Bristol; the Cannington Industrial School boys, "With deep sorrow from the boys of Cannington Industrial School;" "From the Children of Mercy, Holy Cross, Bristol, in mournful remembrance of their consideration by His Lordship;" "From the parishioners of Holy Cross, Bristol, with feelings of deepest sympathy and reverence;" "From the Bristol League of the Cross, in grateful remembrance of generous support and encouragement;" "An offering of respectful gratitude from the Sisters of Mercy, Bristol," and others.

The College bell tolled during the removal of the body from the Mansion, and to-day the half-minute bell sounded as the body was being deposited.

The telegrams received from Pope Leo XIII., before and after the death of the Bishop, were sent from Rome in reply to Monsignor Johnson, secretary to Cardinal Vaughan, Archbishop of Westminster, who wrote from Prior Park. The first, dated Saturday, 12th, was as follows :—

"To Cardinal Vaughan, Archbishop of Westminster. 11.45 Saturday night.—Holy Father sorry for the news; is praying for the Bishop's recovery, and sends him his blessing.

"CARDINAL ROMPOLLER,
"Pontifical Secretary of State."

The second telegram, which arrived after the death of the Bishop, stated:—

"The Holy Father is deeply afflicted at the announcement of the death of the excellent Bishop of Clifton. He will pray for the repose of his blessed soul.

"CARDINAL ROMPOLLER."

APPENDIX NO. I.

I WILL now place before my readers the documents which were drawn up when the changes, to which I have referred, took place at Ampleforth and Prior Park. From their perusal it will be seen that prelates of high distinction and eminent ecclesiastics formed a commission of inquiry and arbitration, and that everything was done legally and terminated to the entire satisfaction of the Commissioners, who spent about six weeks in thoroughly entering into details.

These documents were prefaced as follows :—

"It is well known that, during the last five years, rumours have been widely spread in the Catholic body, importing that various injuries had been inflicted upon the Benedictine Monks by the Vicar Apostolic of the Western District, and particularly that property to a great amount had been unfairly removed from Ampleforth to Prior Park, upon the transfer of the Rev. Messrs. Burgess, Rooker, and Metcalfe from the former to the latter establishment. In justification of his own character and that of the three above-named reverend gentlemen, the Right Rev. Dr. Baines obtained from the Holy See an order that a formal investigation into the truth of these rumours should be made; and the Right Rev. Dr. Briggs, with the Rev. Dr. Youens, on his part, and the Right Rev. Dr. Walsh, with the Very Rev. Charles Brooke,

S.J., on the part of the Benedictine Monks, and the Right Rev. Dr. Scott, chosen by both parties, were accordingly appointed as a commission of inquiry and arbitration. In course of this investigation the two following important documents were produced, not generally known, and which, if made public at first, might have prevented the circulation of injurious reports.

"The first is an agreement between the Rev. Thomas Burgess and others, on the one side, and the Rev. Edward Glover and others, on the other, by which the former, on leaving Ampleforth for Prior Park, agreed to give up everything held by them in trust for the College of Ampleforth, and all the money due to them as Superiors of that establishment; and the latter bound themselves to settle all accounts or debts contracted *bonâ fide* for the said College.

"N.B.—This agreement was drawn up by G. Fielding, Esq., of Northallerton, in Yorkshire, a Catholic of considerable celebrity in his profession, with the mutual consent and approbation of both parties concerned, and runs as follows:—

"AN AGREEMENT made this 13th day of May, 1830, between the Rev. Thomas Burgess, the Rev. Thomas Rooker, and the Rev. Edward Metcalfe, all of Ampleforth, in the county of York, of the one part, and the Rev. Edward Glover, of Little Crosby, in the county of Lancaster, the Rev. Samuel Day, of Clayton Green, of the said county of Lancaster, the Rev. Henry Brewer, of Brownedge, in the said county of Lancaster, and the Rev. Ralph Cooper, of the city of Bath, of the other part, as follows, that is to say, the said Thomas Burgess, Thomas Rooker, and Edward Metcalfe do hereby jointly and severally promise and agree to and with the said Edward Glover, Samuel Day, Henry Brewer, and Ralph Cooper, that they, the said Thomas Burgess, Thomas Rooker, and Edward Metcalfe, and each of them shall and will, upon the request and at the costs and charges of the said Edward Glover, Samuel Day, Henry Brewer, and Ralph Cooper, or the survivors or survivor of them, or the heirs, executors, or administrators of such survivor, execute all such Acts, Deeds, Conveyances, Assignments, Surrenders, Letters of Attorney, and Assurances in the law as the Counsel of the said Edward Glover, Samuel Day, Henry Brewer, and Ralph Cooper, or the survivors or survivor of them, or the heirs, executors, or administrators of such survivor, shall advise or require for conveying, assigning, and transferring unto the said Edward Glover, Samuel Day, Henry Brewer, and Ralph Cooper, their heirs, executors, administrators, and assigns, as joint tenants, according to the nature or quality thereof respectively, subject only to such mortgage or other encumbrances as now affect the same, all the messuages, lands, tenements, and hereditaments of or to which they, the said Thomas Burgess, Thomas Rooker, and Edward Metcalfe, or any or either of them, now are or is seized, possessed, or entitled, situate at Craike, in the county of Durham, Byland, Ampleforth and Oswaldkirk, in the county of York, Orrell Post, in the parish of Wigan, in the county of Lancaster, and Workington, in the county of Cumberland, or elsewhere, in which the said Edward Glover, Samuel Day, Henry Brewer, and Ralph Cooper, or any of them are interested, together with all deeds, evidences, and writings relating thereunto; and also all household goods, furniture, and implements of household, and all farming stock and cattle in and upon the said messuages, lands, tenements, and hereditaments (except the cattle mentioned in the schedule hereunder written, which belong to the said Edward Metcalfe exclusively, and are intended and agreed to be retained by him), and also all monies secured on mortgage, or invested in the funds or upon Government or other securities, in the names of the said Thomas Burgess, Thomas Rooker, and Edward Metcalfe, or any or either of them (other than such monies, if any, as may have been invested in their or any of their names, as a trustee, or trustees, and in which the said Edward Glover, Samuel Day, Henry Brewer, and Ralph Cooper are not beneficially interested). And, further, that until such acts, deeds, assignments, and assurances, as aforesaid, shall be made and executed, they, the said Thomas Burgess, Thomas Rooker, and Edward Metcalfe, their respective heirs, executors, and administrators, shall and will stand and be seized and possessed of all the said premises in trust for the said Edward Glover, Samuel Day, Henry Brewer, and Ralph Cooper, their heirs, executors, administrators, and assigns, as joint tenants. And, for the considerations aforesaid, the said Edward Glover, Samuel Day, Henry

Brewer, and Ralph Cooper do hereby jointly and severally promise and agree to and with the said Thomas Burgess, Thomas Rooker, and Edward Metcalfe, that they, the said Edward Glover, Samuel Day, Henry Brewer, and Ralph Cooper, or some or one of them, shall and will pay and discharge all the sums of money now due and owing by the said Thomas Burgess, Thomas Rooker, and Edward Metcalfe, or any or either of them, which are mentioned and specified in an account stated between the several parties hereto, and this day signed by all of them, and marked with the letter A; and also such other sums of money, if any, as are now due and owing by the said Thomas Burgess, Thomas Rooker, and Edward Metcalfe, or any or either of them, in managing the affairs of Ampleforth College, and shall and will protect and indemnify the said Thomas Burgess, Thomas Rooker, and Edward Metcalfe, and each of them, against all actions, suits, claims, and demands on account thereof. And likewise shall and will, upon or previously to the execution of such conveyance and assignment, as aforesaid, effectually indemnify the said Thomas Burgess, Thomas Rooker, and Edward Metcalfe, and each of them, their respective heirs, executors, and administrators, against the payment of the mortgage debt and other encumbrances affecting the messuages and other hereditaments herein before mentioned, or any part thereof, and against all actions, suits, claims, and demands on account of the same.

"Witness our hands,

"Signed by the said Thomas Burgess, Thomas Rooker, Edward Metcalfe, Edward Glover, and Samuel Day, in the presence of
JOHN BIRDSALL.

THOMAS BURGESS.
THOMAS ROOKER.
EDWARD METCALFE.
EDWARD GLOVER.
SAMUEL DAY.

"Signed by the said Henry Brewer, in the presence of
EDWARD CLIFFORD.

HENRY BREWER.

"Signed by the said Ralph Cooper, in the presence of
JOSEPH SPENCER.

RALPH COOPER."

After this and on the same sheet of paper is written the schedule of the cattle, and the prices at which they were valued to Dr. Baines and paid for by him to the College of Ampleforth, amounting in all to £797 2s.

This valuation was made by Mr. Hunter, a respectable farmer in the neighbourhood of the College, and agreed to by both parties. These are the cattle which report said were forcibly and fraudulently taken away.

So well were the four Commissioners for the Benedictine body—viz., the Very Rev. John Birdsall, President-General of the English Benedictine Congregation, the Rev. Richard Marsh, the Rev. Thomas Robinson, and the Rev. Edward Glover—satisfied with the conduct of the Rev. Thomas Burgess, the Rev. Thomas Rooker, and the Rev. Edward Metcalfe, that the morning after the above agreement had been signed the Very Rev. John

Birdsall put the following memorandum into the hands of the Rev. Thomas Burgess, enclosing a cheque for £30, as a viaticum to Prior Park for himself and the Rev. Messrs. Rooker and Metcalfe.

N.B.—As this memorandum and viaticum were given the day after the above deed was signed, and the deed was signed without any other conditions but those therein expressed, the giving this memorandum and viaticum was a perfectly voluntary act on the part of those who gave it, and expressive of their feelings at the time.

The following is a faithful copy of the original memorandum, and is the second document referred to above :—

Memorandum.

"That upon the retirement of the Rev. Thomas Burgess, Thomas Rooker, and Edward Metcalfe from our body, in consequence of the indult obtained by them from Rome, they received at the time of surrender of the property into the hands of the Rev. Edward Glover, the Superior *pro tempore* of our establishment at that place, £30, as a viaticum for their journey to Prior Park, over and above the balance of the accounts delivered in.

"And that, in consideration of their labours during the years of their being members of our body, it was given them to understand that, notwithstanding their separation from us, we shall be prepared to afford them the same assistance and means of comfort, attention being had to that portion of their lives spent amongst us, as is customary with us to render to our own brethren, when age, infirmity, or necessity came upon them.

"EDWARD GLOVER.
"RICHARD MARSH.
"THOMAS ROBINSON.
"AUG. JOHN BIRDSALL, Præs. Gen.

"Ampleforth College, May 13th, 1830."

After a full investigation into every particular, a detailed report was sent, as ordered, to Rome, to the Sacred Congregation of Propaganda, for its authoritative sanction. In the meantime the following document was drawn up by the above-named Right Rev. and Rev. Commissioners, and delivered to the Right Rev. Dr. Baines, as a justification before the public of himself and friends.

[*Copy.*]

"It appears to the Arbitrators that no part of the property of the Monastery of Ampleforth was taken away by Messrs. Burgess, Metcalfe, and Rooker, nor received by Dr. Baines, except a picture of St. Jerome, which was removed under an erroneous impression that it had been given to Mr. Burgess; and a sum of about £150, which was taken through an unintentional error; which error having been discovered by Mr. Burgess, during the course of this inquiry, that sum has been repaid by him. Of these mistakes, Dr. Baines could not have had any knowledge.

"The Arbitrators further add, in general terms, that in the course of their inquiries they have not met with anything to impeach the character of either Dr. Baines, or of Messrs. Burgess, Metcalfe, and Rooker.

"THOMAS WALSH, V.A.
"ANDREW SCOTT, V.A.
"JOHN BRIGGS.
"THOMAS YOUENS.
"CHARLES BROOKE.

"Clifton, 22nd August, 1835."

N.B.—The picture of St. Jerome was not removed from Ampleforth till the donor thereof had been consulted, whether it was a personal gift to Prior Burgess, or a gift to the College. The donor's answer was faithfully reported to the Very Rev. Mr. Birdsall and the other Commissioners at the time of the final settlement, May 13th, 1830; and they, in consequence thereof, allowed this picture to be entered amongst the other things to be taken away by Prior Burgess. It was not, therefore, taken away either clandestinely or fraudulently, as was reported; but the donor having since intimated that his answer was misunderstood, and that he wished the picture to remain at Ampleforth, it is given up.

The second mistake, regarding the sum of about £150, originated in certain notes of hand not having been paid into the College, which Mr. Burgess thought had been paid in, when he made up the accounts betwixt Dr. Baines and the English Benedictine Monks. The interest arising from these notes having been mixed up with the receipts for rents of some houses, since 1823, caused this oversight to be made; but being discovered by Prior Burgess in looking over the accounts in the late investigation, he was empowered by Dr. Baines to rectify the mistake. Prior Burgess only acted as accomptant for the parties in this affair.

After the conclusion of this Synod, as a public act of friendship and open testimony of satisfaction at the result of this investigation, the Right Rev. and Rev. Arbitrators dined with both parties at Prior Park, and the day following at Downside College. *Et sic finitur ad majorem Dei gloriam.*

APPENDIX NO. II.

MR. THOMAS THOMPSON AT PRIOR PARK.

IT may perhaps prove of some interest to learn what became of the College after its closure—during a period of eleven years and four months.

On the first day of the year 1856, legal proceedings were taken by Mr. Raphael, and the property of Prior Park was sold, as I have said, by public auction. In September, 1859, nearly four years after, Mr. Thompson rented the Mansion, and remained there until his death, which occurred on the 8th of December, 1865—a period of about six years and three months. He had resided at Lansdown Crescent, but it was not to his taste. There was no privacy or freedom, and little of that picturesque beauty in which he delighted. He had cast a longing eye on Prior Park, which had been for some years on sale and untenanted. The exquisitely beautiful view, unique of its kind, and the sweet seclusion of its walks in the grounds were no small attractions. His imagination exulted in the idea of the happy children who might, in summer time, partake of his pleasure, and of the meetings, for many good and benevolent objects, which might be held in the Park. The month of May came, the first May he enjoyed at Prior Park. No time was lost for carrying out his purposes, for the gratification of the poor and their children. Through his whole life, he had always been a large contributor to children's treats. He had often planned and started them, and had, not unfrequently, given them at his sole cost; but he had never before had the same scope or facilities for gratifying his benevolent impulses. For five successive summers, he realised in large measure the happiness so congenial to his nature—that of making others happy. During the fine weather, schools and gatherings of poor people, from Bath and the neighbouring districts, came, on an average, two or three afternoons in each week. Preference of sect was not thought of. Church of England, Countess of Huntingdon, Independent and Baptist, Wesleyan and Primitive Methodist, Orphan and Ragged, Reformatory and Training Schools, and Workhouse children—who, by the way, received special attention—all came in turn. The Bands of Hope and Temperance Alliance sometimes assembled in numbers of from one to three thousand, and on one occasion to a much greater extent. Very pleasant it was to him to see them marching in, with happy faces, in holiday attire, and pausing to sing their hymns or pieces under his study window. The terraces and sloping greensward below, the walks and vacant Colleges adjoining the house, were all thrown open for the day, and in joyous abandonment the children sported on the lawns, whilst their seniors wandered through the shady walks or spacious buildings. Preparations were always made for the school children. Hot water for making tea was provided on a large scale in the house, and the servants entered into the spirit of their master, and were ever ready to afford their help. He and Mrs. Thompson went out to receive the children, and to welcome the teachers individually. He provided amusements, suggested games, and joined heartily in the children's play. The strongest muster and the greatest fun always gathered around him; and it was not until the last two years of his life that he ceased to take his turn in running or jumping with the little ones. As the evening drew on, they assembled on the steps or under the magnificent portico of the Mansion, to sing their closing hymn and to listen to their host's parting words. As they passed, in single file, through the noble hall to the south exit, each one received from him a little book in remembrance of the day. The number of meetings held at Prior Park would seem almost fabulous; and Mr. Thomas Thompson seems to have improved every opportunity of doing good in his way and of showing kindness to all who came.

During this time the Clifton School, established by Bishop Clifford and conducted by Dr. Williams and his brother James, had been progressing, and its inmates could no longer be accommodated on the existing premises. Dr. Williams, thus compelled to make a change, considered that his School was of sufficient importance to warrant his taking up his position at St. Paul's College, Prior Park, and he fixed his heart on doing so. Speaking to me on the subject, Dr. Williams said, "I considered the matter over three days and three nights, and each day my desire to go to Prior Park grew stronger. I then consulted His

Lordship, Bishop Clifford, who, seeing that I was in good earnest, said very little, but did much." In less than three months, such arrangements were made as enabled the School at Clifton to become the College at Prior Park.

The 23rd of April, 1867, is a day to be remembered in the annals of Prior Park. On that day, Dr. Williams and his brother, with their staff of Professors and the students, took possession of a long-lost Catholic inheritance. On that day, the fruits of the labours and anxieties, endured by many and devoted servants of God and the Church, were rescued from oblivion and restored to posterity. On that day, the sun shone in splendour on Prior Park, as on its resurrection morn. On that day, Prior Park College rose, as it were, from the tomb of oblivion in which it had rested for more than eleven years, and, casting off its shroud of debts and encumbrances, renewed its youth, and now, after twenty-six years of manly struggles to hold its own, finds itself intellectually and financially working on a sound and solid basis.

Some interesting presentations were made to the new College. The large picture, by Van Dyke, of the Crucifixion, now hanging in the Mansion Chapel, had been purchased by Hugh Bateman, Esq. (for many years a student), for £472. This he generously presented to the College.

The Benedictines of Downside had purchased at the sale the portrait of Dr. Baines and that of Leo XII., and with graceful courtesy, which was much appreciated, replaced them in the position which they had previously occupied in St. Paul's.

APPENDIX NO. III.

The Priory.

SINCE the arrangements made by the Trustees of the College with Mr. Bryant, the Priory with its grounds has risen in importance. Its value has been greatly increased, and its beauty and picturesqueness enhanced—so much so that there is a general desire to know something of its history.

Its name, "Priory," is suggestive of having belonged to the Benedictine Monastery and Abbey of Bath. But on inquiry, though it stands on the land which belonged to the Priors of Bath, the building itself does not date so far back, for it was built by Ralph Allen, as a residence for his steward.

The original Priory was down at the ponds, which seen from the portico are like lakes, and add very much to the beauty of the surrounding scenery. The present College laundry was the ancient residence of the Priors of Bath, though it is now in a mutilated form; for Ralph Allen removed from it all that was ornamental and architectural, and worked it into the building which is now called the Priory, and which is the residence of Mr. Bryant and his family.

Though the present Bath Abbey is not remarkable for its antiquity, as are the cathedrals of England in general, still it occupies a site which, from the first establishment of Christianity in this part of the country, has been consecrated to religious uses.

The Saxon King Offa, in the year 775, built the first church there, which it is said was destroyed by the Danes. Other buildings followed with chequered fortunes, until in the year 1160 a Norman Cathedral with round arches not only covered the site of the present Abbey, but extended its chancel as far as the railings of the Institution Gardens.

At this time there was a Prior of Bath, and he and the monks constituted the Bishop's Chapter. I am not prepared to say whether the Priors of Bath at that period had a priory country residence at the laundry; but it is within the range of possibilities, for the building is ancient. In the year 1515 we are told that Prior W. Bird laid the first stone of his oratory in the Bath Abbey, when the Abbey was in Catholic hands. The so-called ecclesiastical reforms were following close upon this; and we may presume that Prior Bird was the last Prior of Bath who lived at his country house near the ponds of Prior Park. When Prior Park became a College, the Priory was the dormitory of the elder students, and Dr. Logan, Dr. Toomey, and other Professors had their rooms there. As soon as rooms were prepared in the Mansion and in St. Paul's, the Priory was vacated, and the Hon. Miss Crewe took possession of it. After the fire in 1836 Dr. Baines resided for a short time there, during the restoration of the Mansion.

Mr. Henry Knight, of Cannington, and his son and daughter resided there for a short time. His son Thomas was a student at Prior Park, and became a very advanced pupil of Mr. Henry Field, the eminent pianist of Bath, of whom mention has already been made. Mr. Charles Welman and his family also occupied the Priory, previously to its being leased for 21 years to G. R. Bryant, Esq.

Without interfering with the main features of the Priory, Mr. Bryant has enlarged the building so as to suit the requirements of a large family; and any villa more beautifully decorated and furnished, and more convenient and picturesque, it would be difficult to find even in the beautiful surroundings of Bath.

The grounds, too, have undergone a marvellous change, and the terraces lying one below the other are admirably adapted for outdoor amusements.

At the dissolution the site of the Bath Abbey was granted to Humphrey Collis, who afterwards disposed of it to Matthew Colethurst. His son Edmund presented the Abbey Church, which was then become ruinous (having been stripped of its lead, glass, iron, and bells), to the Mayor and citizens of Bath, for their parochial church. He sold the Abbey House, with the park called Prior Park, to Fulk Morley, from whose descendants the estate devolved through the Duke of Kingston to Lord Newark, and later through the Allens to Lord Hawarden.

In "Dugdale's British Traveller" mention is made of a large and deep fosse called Wansdike. It commenced at Andover, in Hampshire, and crossed the Avon at Bathampton, and thence continued its course over Claverton Down to Prior Park, and terminated in the Severn sea at Portishead, a distance of eighty miles from its commencement. I have never heard of any of our Prior Park pedestrians having found any traces of the Wansdike at Claverton Down or Prior Park. But Mr. Bryant, who now resides at the Priory, informs me that at one of his former residences in the direction of Chippenham he could distinctly trace the remains of the dike, and that a house near him went by the name of Wansdike House. The origin of the dike was as follows :—

About the commencement of the Christian Era, Divitiacus, King of the Suessones, brought over a considerable army from the continent to assist his countrymen, who had migrated hither and were at war with the natives. The incessant hostilities were then appeased ; a treaty was concluded ; and a line was drawn to determine their respective boundaries. The Wansdike fosse constituted the boundary here spoken of, and is interesting to us inasmuch as it passed over the Prior Park grounds. On Marlborough Downs this singular dike appears in its pristine state, being exceedingly deep, and flanked by a lofty mound.

The Reminiscences and account of the buildings must end here, and the writer trusts his readers have acquired some interesting information from perusing them. Many details have of necessity been passed over, but the main outlines of his account are reliable. Let each reader draw his own moral from the "men and measures" of which some notice has been given, and may the many exemplars of past generations of the College ever be repeating themselves in the present and future ones. History and biography are bracing, because they are so emphatically human. God grant that the future history of Prior Park College may give additional force and renewed zest to the principles upon which "former lights" of the College strove, and not unsuccessfully, to do whatever their hands found to do in the world around them.

PROSPECTUS.

COLLEGES OF SS. PETER AND PAUL, PRIOR PARK, NEAR BATH.

THESE Colleges consist of a central building and two wings, joined together both by covered passages and open arcades. They are beautifully situated at the head of the Vale of Widcombe, overlooking the City of Bath, from which they are distant about a mile and a half. The Park and pleasure grounds are about thirty acres in extent, and stand nearly in the centre of the estate.

The Colleges and Chapel are warmed on the hot water system. A Lavatory of the newest and most perfect kind, with bath-room annexed, has just been constructed in the Junior College. It opens out of the dormitories, and is supplied with both hot and cold water. The Hot Water Swimming Bath, 60 feet of water by 25, is now in use. No expense has been spared in fitting up these and other important parts of the house with everything that health and comfort can require.

The younger boys are in St. Peter's College, to the east of the Mansion ; St. Paul's, which forms the western wing, contains the elder students. They have separate play-grounds, but the same Refectory and Chapel. Each wing has a Boys' Library and Reading Room.

The Drill Sergeant attends weekly. The President and Masters take their meals in the Refectory with the Boys.

The Year, exclusive of the Vacations, is divided into three Terms of Fourteen Weeks each; the first beginning on the 15th January, the second on the 23rd April, and the third on the 17th September.

The Vacations are from the 30th July to the 17th September, and from the 22nd December to the 15th January. Students may remain at the College during the Vacations on the payment of £1 10s. per week.

Cheques and Orders to be made payable to the Very Rev. Monsignor Williams.

Students, whose parents live in the neighbourhood, will be allowed to go home on the Monthly Holiday.

ST. PETER'S COLLEGE.

Prefect:

Very Rev. Charles H. Canon Collingridge.

In this College a thorough preparation is aimed at in the earlier stages of Education, so as to enable the Students, when they pass into St. Paul's, to pursue the higher studies with success. A Matron looks after the health and cleanliness of the little Boys, and the building is fitted up with special attention to their requirements and comforts.

The Pension in St. Peter's College for Boys over ten years of age is 17 Guineas a Term;

for Boys under ten, or for Brothers of any age, 16 Guineas a Term, payable in advance. Music and Drawing, each, Two Guineas a Term. Subscription to the Public Games (the Cricket Club, the Gymnasium, Football, and Tennis), One Guinea a Year.

St. Paul's College.

Prefect: Rev. Joseph Chard.

This College is intended for the more advanced classes. Each Student has a separate bedroom. A complete liberal education is given, embracing Greek, Latin, English, German, and French Languages, Ancient and Modern History, Geography, Mathematics, Book-keeping, Natural Philosophy, Chemistry, etc.

The course of study is adapted as far as possible to the demands of the various public examinations.

The Pension in St. Paul's College is 20 Guineas a Term. For Brothers, 19 Guineas a Term. Music and Drawing, each, Two Guineas a Term. Subscription to the Public Games (the Cricket Club, Gymnasium, Football, and Tennis), £1 5s. a Year. *There are no extras.*

The Mansion.

Students for the Church are accommodated in the Mansion, which is warmed with hot-water pipes. The heat pervades the lofty hall and Chapel, and reaches the upper rooms, imparting a dry and healthy atmosphere to the whole building.

The Philosophical and Theological studies are conducted by the Very Rev. Father Isles, B.D., of Louvain. Every opportunity is afforded to them of acquiring a good style of Pulpit Oratory, by the Very Rev. Monsignor Shepherd, Professor of Elocution in the Colleges. Foreigners have been very successful under him in acquiring, in an unusually short period of time, a perfect English pronunciation. Reference is kindly permitted to former French pupils—Messrs. Deneck, Despretz, Leclerc, of Lille.

CPSIA information can be obtained
at www.ICGtesting.com
Printed in the USA
BVHW041045190619
551408BV00030B/1879/P

9 781166 163181